SHOMIE DAS

The Man Who Saw Tomorrow

SHOMIE DAS

The Man Who Saw Tomorrow

NAGA TUMMALA

Foreword by Rudrangshu Mukherjee

Om Books International

First published in 2024 by

Om Books International

Corporate & Editorial Office
A-12, Sector 64, Noida 201 301
Uttar Pradesh, India
Phone: +91 120 477 4100
Email: editorial@ombooks.com
Website: www.ombooksinternational.com

Sales Office
107, Ansari Road, Darya Ganj,
New Delhi 110 002, India
Phone: +91 11 4000 9000
Email: sales@ombooks.com
Website: www.ombooks.com

ISBN: 978-93-63956-40-7

Printed in India

10 9 8 7 6 5 4 3 2 1

Dedicated to all teachers and educators tirelessly shaping future generations to be learned, progressive, and happier, and to all well-meaning individuals striving to impact the world of education.

Contents

Foreword

I should begin with a full disclosure. Shomie Das is my uncle-in-law. His didi (elder sister) is my mother-in-law, though if truth be told she treated me more as a son than a son-in-law. Shomie and I have known each other from 1973–74 when I had just finished my undergraduate degree in history from Presidency College, Calcutta, and Shomie was the headmaster of Mayo College. I must confess that through some ineffable chemistry we got along very well from the first time we met. One reason for this, I think, is the fact that Shomie didn't allow the age difference and formality to stand in the way of our evolving relationship. From my side, my attitude towards him was not without a healthy dose of respect and admiration.

Shomie, after having studied physics at St. Xavier's College, Calcutta, and Emmanuel College, Cambridge, chose to become a schoolteacher. Some of my admiration for him stemmed from this decision of his very early on in his career. I have heard from some of Shomie's former pupils that he was an excellent classroom teacher. Shomie himself has told me that he missed teaching when he became headmaster of Mayo, Lawrence School, Sanawar, and Doon and was forced to reduce his teaching load. The loss of a good teacher was more than compensated by Shomie's role as an institution builder.

This book is about the building of an institution, Oakridge School, in present-day Telangana, and of Shomie's lifelong commitment to school education. Most people mouth the cliché that today's children are tomorrow's future. Shomie walked that talk and devoted his life to educating children and to building institutions which would enable that education.

I must emphasize here that Shomie's ideas about education transcend the conventional notion of what education is about. Shomie has never believed that education is only about doing well in examinations. His ideas go to the root of the word—the Latin *educere*, to draw out. He is passionate about opening the doors and windows of young minds, to stoke their curiosity and to expand their intellectual landscape. Education, for Shomie, has never been transactional. This is the primary reason why he commands so much respect and loyalty from so many of his former pupils from all the three schools that he led from the front. There are many anecdotes and recollections in this book that reinforce the point I am making.

In a private conversation Shomie once told me—and I hope he will not mind my retelling this—that he believed that his best years as an educationist were his Sanawar years. I was a bit surprised. I had expected he would say Doon, which in more ways than one was a homecoming for him. When I articulated my surprise, Shomie explained that by the time he came to Doon as headmaster, he no longer had the energy that had driven him to completely transform Sanawar. I was quite taken aback by his candid self-reflection. My respect for him went up a few notches. Reading this book, I have come to the conclusion that the Oakridge project had given Shomie a kind of second wind. He got another chance to innovate and to implement some of his ideas. The heavy hand of tradition in Doon had perhaps not quite given Shomie the space and the opportunity to do that.

This book is the story of the interface between two entrepreneurs, Naga Prasad Tummala and Rajasekhar Yarlagadda, and a dedicated educationist. It has many stories and many lessons. While I am not sure that Shomie is prescient, what I am certain about, having known Shomie for nearly five decades, is that he is someone who is committed to tomorrow. Very few, even the best amongst us, have that commitment. Age has not withered that intensity in Shomie.

RUDRANGSHU MUKHERJEE
CHANCELLOR AND PROFESSOR OF HISTORY
ASHOKA UNIVERSITY
27 APRIL 2024

Section I

Education: A Journey

1

The Beginning

"We do not remember days, we remember moments."
—Cesare Pavese

I shuffled in my seat, readjusting the bag strap that was weighing down on my shoulder. Raj was to my left, peering out of the window. Dhanunjaya was to my right. It was a hot Tuesday afternoon in Dehradun. We were a long way from home.

The three of us had arrived in Dehradun early on Sunday after a thirty-two-hour train journey. Partners in an education enterprise, we had travelled north as part of our explorative school visits. Although we had already spent seven years in this field, we were about to undertake a different level of challenge. Our goal for this next venture was simple yet gargantuan: we wanted to transform the landscape of education in India.

To many in the year 2000, this mission seemed both trivial and baffling. There wasn't an obvious need for a seismic shift in pedagogy, so why would this trio of small-town entrepreneurs task themselves with such a mammoth goal? People couldn't envision the future of schooling that we were hoping to create, but they wished us well. And since the masses were not ready to embrace this change, we were in the pursuit of a revolutionary mind that would.

Until our frontman could be found, we had other duties to address. With a solemn belief that every institution offered something for us to learn, we set our sights on as many schools within reach. Most times, school office bearers would welcome us and graciously entertain our inquisitions. Other times, to avoid being seen as competition, we would take on the guise of prospective parents seeking to enrol our children.

Here in Dehradun, there were four stops on our planned tour. The first was the Brightlands School in Dalanwala, which had marked our opening visit on Monday. We met the principal, who generously gave us a tour of their quaint campus. As a family-run school, teachers and staff fondly recalled their association with the founder, the late Mrs Narang, and her son, Ravi Narang. It may have been a smaller enterprise, but they were rewarded with an uplifting sense of community.

After lunch, we had surveyed the Summer Valley School. Founded in 1994, it was a relatively nascent institution, and their journey foreshadowed some of the challenges we would probably encounter. From infrastructure to classroom density, we took note of their struggles and successes in effectively engaging and personalizing education for their students.

At the end of the evening, Raj, Dhanunjaya and I were seated on a bench on Jaipur Road, drinking chhaas and trading our observations from the day. I outlined my takeaways from their management styles whereas Raj and Dhanunjaya pondered on the comparative scale of their facilities. We agreed that the culture of learning felt more evolved in this city, but we were not yet prepared for what day two would bring.

On Tuesday morning, we had checked out of our hotel after breakfast and headed to the Welham Girls' School. We had to board an evening train back to Delhi, and as such the schedule was tight. Leaving our bags in the admin block, we traversed the grounds. Diving into the rich history of their establishment, we were amazed to discover that since its inception in 1957, the school had been spearheaded by a lineage of brilliant women in leadership.

That undoubtedly reflected in the overall tenor of Welham. It felt tight-knit and distinguished but did not stray from Indian traditions and their roots. Raj and I even wondered out loud if this indomitable spirit could be recreated elsewhere. And as esteemed as Welham was in its own right, we were looking forward to exploring the even deeper traditions of an older institution in town, a ten-minute taxi ride away.

When we stepped out of the cab, all three of us fell silent. We strode through the rusty arched gates and made our way to the main quad, immediately feeling enclosed and simultaneously distant to the world outside. The afternoon sun was beating down hard against the red brick exteriors and dense foliage, but it still looked majestic. We had arrived at the final stop on our trip: The Doon School.

As an all-boys' boarding school that had its genesis in 1930s' British India, Doon was a veritable spectacle. We started off with a guided tour during the first hour, which didn't nearly convey its full magnitude – a vast and immersive campus, spread over 70 acres, with an unparalleled atmosphere. From the Kilachand Library to the Rose Bowl amphitheatre, each element of its infrastructure enmeshed with the surrounding natural environs truly set the school apart.

It was brought to life, of course, by the students who huddled in the corridors and played on the grounds. I watched young lads file in and out of buildings, dressed to the nines in grey blazers and slacks, the school emblem proudly emblazoned on their chests. Interestingly, there were no more than 500 pupils on this expansive estate, especially since Doon only taught grades 7-12. This ensured a close kinship, the tour guide mentioned, as boarders of all ages studied and lived together in school houses.

From the teachers, we learnt that Doon's mission has long been both idealistic and egalitarian. The school aims to serve a meritocratic India, wherein their students develop strong competence, leadership and ethics during their time as "Doscos". We also witnessed first-hand their touted sentiment of being "an aristocracy of service", which was supplemented with a culture and approach that exuded a distinct sense of elitism. They produce the intellectual crème de la crème, making Doon one of the finest schools in India.

After leaving the campus we stopped at The English Book Depot, a cafe and bookstore, on our way to the station. Placing three orders for cappuccino, we split down the aisles and soaked in the blended aroma of coffee and old books, some of them over eighty years old. The magic of Doon lingered in the air.

The Meeting

Raj and I concurred that our visit to The Doon School was easily the most remarkable. As Dhanunjaya rattled off a myriad of reasons that lend to its prestige, he broached one particular factoid that caused our ears to perk up. He had heard during the tour that a former headmaster of the school still lived in Dehradun and consulted on the G.D. Goenka School advisory board. Our friend had even managed to ask for his phone number.

Intrigued by the wealth of knowledge that this man could share, I decided it was at least worth a call. Rushing out to the nearest payphone, I dialled his residence and breathed heavily as the line rang. I realized in that moment that I didn't know much about this stranger beyond his name.

"Hello?" The line clicked open.

I cleared my throat. "Mr Shomie Das?"

"Yes, and who am I speaking to?" He paused, his voice as soothing as it was commanding.

"Hello, sir, my name is Naga Prasad."

After I introduced myself and my business partners, I let him know that we had just visited the school and found it fascinating. I even expressed our own plans to start a school in the south, and our vision for its growth.

"Are you still here in Dehradun?" he asked without missing a beat.

"Yes, sir," I answered, rolling my wrist to look at the time.

"Why don't you come by my house? We can talk more then," he suggested.

I glanced at Raj and Dhanunjaya who stood outside the booth, mouthing his offer to them. Raj instinctively yanked out the train tickets from his shirt pocket and ripped them in half. He was a bit theatrical that way. Accepting the offer, I ended the call and followed Mr Das's directions to his home in Clement Town. That is how the three of us found ourselves in this stuffy cab on a hot September day.

When we reached our destination, I hopped off with our belongings and led us to his place. It was a charming double-storeyed home surrounded by neatly manicured lawns and shrubbery. We marched up to the door and rang the bell, only to be immediately met with alarming barks. As their help opened the door, a young Labrador pounced at my legs and began clawing for attention. I bent down to pet her as a hoarse voice called out. "That's enough, Saachi."

Before us stood a man in his mid-sixties, the whites in his beard and hair clearly betraying his age. His small stature was offset by his firm stance and the thick bronze-rimmed glasses perched on his nose bridge. He smiled and greeted us warmly. After he introduced us to his lovely wife, Pheroza Das, we sat in the living room and munched on some snacks. The overtone was oddly comfortable and familiar, as though we were visiting an old college professor of ours.

What I thought would be a brief chat lasted for hours. We were enchanted by Shomie's achievements, of which there were many. Not only had he studied at The Doon School back in the day, but his grandfather, Satish Ranjan Das, was the original founder. Shomie had later graduated from St Xavier's College in Calcutta as Kolkata was known then, and then studied at the University of Cambridge. I think Raj and I will forever remember how casually he mentioned that he had taught King Charles III during his time at the Gordonstoun School in Scotland.

Shomie's superlative background aside, I was especially charmed by who he was as an intellectual and as a person. We found common ground on several guiding principles that would shape our own endeavour. On matters where we pushed with callow eagerness, he countered with sage experience. He could clearly articulate the failings of the Indian education system or identify areas for scholastic reform, but he could do all that and more with a charisma that made all the difference.

Shomie was a seasoned academician. After serving as headmaster at two other eminent institutions, the Mayo College and the Lawrence School, Sanawar, he was spending his time now by consulting for over fifty schools across the country. Notwithstanding his exclusive pedigree, the empathy and keenness he felt for the generations of students ahead resonated loudly through his words and actions. He was a man who could see tomorrow.

As he escorted us to the door and we said our goodbyes, I had only one word on my mind.

Frontman.

An Enterprise of Collaboration

So that was how it all started. In Dehradun. A conversation that began just by chance. A spur-of-the-moment phone call. Train tickets ripped up in the anticipation of something that could be a game changer. But who are these people? Rajasekhar Yarlagadda, Dhanunjaya, Shomie Das and me, Naga Prasad.

For the purpose of this story, Raj and I are childhood friends turned entrepreneurs and partners with a shared interest: education. To be more specific, education with a difference.

Dhanunjaya was our third partner at that point.

And Shomie Das? To put it in a nutshell, he is the man who gave shape to Raj's and my dream of founding a school where education was not only a system of teaching but also a unique experience. Shomie was the inspiration and also the idea that led to that experience.

That was how Oakridge School in Hyderabad, modern-day Telangana, was born. We have since exited Oakridge. But it is the idea that is important; how a man with a vision can make a difference, and how two committed entrepreneurs can turn that vision into reality. This book is a tribute to that collaborative enterprise, of idea and effort, between two young men in their thirties and an elderly retired man "steeped in education".

What follows is an account of that partnership and what it achieved. It will take you not just through our story and the stories behind the story, but also how the education landscape in India has changed over the years, through the eyes of perhaps India's most distinguished educator.

Apart from education, there's a key takeaway from the book: the mutual respect between the educationist with the vision and the facilitators of that vision, all the more remarkable considering the difference in contexts and years.

Raj and I both come from rural backgrounds in the southern coastal state of Andhra Pradesh, where existence revolves largely around the fecundity of earth and yield. But the seeds of education were probably sown early since my father ran a school in the small town of Nuzvid where we lived.

The two of us would later shift to Visakhapatnam, a burgeoning port town, where we started Vikas, a residential junior college, which would go on to become one of the top institutes.

But Visakhapatnam eventually became too limited for Raj and I and we shifted base to Hyderabad. It was not an easy choice and at times, with little returns and mounting debts, we weren't sure what the day after would bring. But we hung on, convincing our financiers to back us, but more important, backing ourselves in situations that would have unnerved most. It was this determination that impressed Shomie.

A scientist at heart, Shomie says he was never a brilliant student, in the traditional sense of the term, but he went on to become a great teacher, evident from all the schools he has headed, and bringing about changes within the system.

The one passion that drove him – and still does at a remarkably sprightly eighty-eight years young – was how to make the scholastic lives of students more interesting; how to make them curious, to question without unthinking acceptance and to reason. He is totally against the rote system of learning and would experiment a lot and, quite often, with positive results. Not that it was easy, especially in a system long habituated to the old ways. But he went ahead, anyway. In a way, therefore, his chance meeting with Raj and me, several years into his retirement from Doon School, ensured a continuation of the ideas he had explored as a teacher – but this time with more freedom.

Looking back on our journey together, Raj and I thank the gods above that we didn't catch the train from Dehradun to Delhi that afternoon. Destiny works in strange ways – sometimes through impulsive acts like tearing up train tickets.

2

A Meeting of Minds

It was the beginning of the year 2000. A new decade, and the threshold of a new millennium. My partner Raj and I were buoyant with plans to establish what we referred to then simply as a "good" school. We did not know what a "good" school meant. Or even what we meant by it. But we took the time to learn.

As part of our research, as mentioned before, we had already embarked on a School Yatra of sorts, visiting schools across cities and even countries. Our intent was simple: to understand what made some of those schools outstanding, and why others failed. Doon School, with its distinguished history, featured prominently on our itinerary. And so, we set off to visit the school with Dhanunjaya.

When we arrived at the school, its colonial grandeur set amidst lush lawns and its atmosphere of industrious serenity was overwhelming, given our simple backgrounds. The gentleman showing us around explained that Doon School was born when one Satish Ranjan Das decided to establish a school along the lines of British public schools. He felt this was required to nurture future citizens of a free India who could take over the reins of the nation's administration once the British left. We were wonderstruck at the vision of that gentleman because his foresight was definitely not ordinary.

Imagine, then, our interest when we heard that a previous headmaster of the school, Shomie Ranjan Das, was the grandson of the same Satish Ranjan Das. And that, after retiring, he was acting as a consultant helping to establish new schools, one being the G.D. Goenka School in Delhi. That Shomie Das was from such an illustrious family, had been headmaster of the Doon School, had just retired from active service and was helping to set up new schools piqued our interest and, as Raj always says, almost "seemed to be a sign from the Universe".

Young and impulsive, yet seasoned entrepreneurs already, we were used to acting decisively as well as listening to our gut. So, we set about figuring out how to meet *the* Shomie Das. The gentleman showing us around had shared Das's phone number, the information that he lived in Dehradun, but not much more.

Remember, in those days mobile phones did not have roaming facilities. However, phone booths were ubiquitous. So, as I have written before, to a phone booth we went and rang Shomie up. Luckily, he had just returned from a trip and he asked us to come over.

As just narrated, we were scheduled to leave Dehradun in the next couple of hours. But something told us to postpone our return and meet this gentleman. When Shomie welcomed us in, we were already in awe of his surroundings. His house was fascinating – colonial in architecture, very conspicuously English in design. I had not visited any such house before this.

Mind you, it was not a mansion, not even a palatial bungalow. It was not ostentatious in any way. Call it aesthetics, call it atmosphere but the interiors spoke of a life of the intellect, of curiosity and of cultured grace.

As Raj, Dhanunjaya and I settled down, the conversation flowed. We told Shomie that we wanted to start a school and shared our ideas. As the discussion continued – for almost three to four hours – we realized that this gentleman held all the knowledge we needed to make our dream of setting up a "good" school come true. At that point, we felt that God had created an opportunity for us to work with him. And the first action point was to convince him to come on board.

Initially, Shomie was not very confident about what we could or would do. We told him that we had visited close to a hundred schools within the country and some outside India to understand what makes a good school. We told him we wished to engage his services as advisor because he had the knowledge and experience that we lacked. However, Shomie just thanked us courteously, wished us well and that was it. End of discussion.

We were undeterred, though. Remember we were entrepreneurs, used to risks and challenges. We returned to Visakhapatnam, with the firm belief that Shomie Das was the person we needed. The challenge was to actualize and operationalize that engagement. It was impossible to move ahead with just that one interaction in Dehradun. So, after a few days, we called Shomie to ask him if he was willing to come over for further discussions. He was, however, reluctant as at that time he was helping a school in Kolkata and, thus, travelling frequently. We were also quite sure that if we could just get him to visit us and see the work we were doing, he would be more convinced about our ability to deliver such a project. We saw that there was one direct flight from Kolkata to Visakhapatnam and managed to persuade him to fly down from Kolkata. He did come down, maybe because he was too courteous to refuse. The rest, as they say, is history!

What about the other side of that history-making meeting? What about Shomie Das's impressions?

Believe me when I say that we – and several others – have asked Shomie this same question umpteen times. He always replies with his usual charming candour, "After retiring, I had met many promoters. Almost too many. They always came with fixed ideas and fixed expectations from me. They would say, 'I am going to build an ICSE school. You do it for me.' These two, though, were noticeably different. First, they were very young, in their early thirties. I did not think that they would have the money to build even a small school. So, I gave them a challenge. I promised that I would certainly help them get the IB affiliation, provided they fulfilled the basic parameters and criteria. I was quite sure that that was the last I would see of them. Not because they were not in earnest. They were clearly serious. But they were young and they did not know all the pitfalls."

But this was one time the "teacherly" ability to read people failed Shomie. A combination of earnestness, dedication, appetite for risks and just maybe our youth meant that we did not know enough to be afraid. And as Shomie puts it so beautifully, we "dived into the project, heart first".

The exchange was not all one-sided, though. We brought to the table a lot of knowledge and insights about setting up enterprises. The combination was set for success. But this is only on paper. As Shomie says, what actually made it work was not only his expertise and experience but our enthusiasm and our committed, unquestioning trust. Not that we didn't or don't disagree – we do even today. This is what he has to say about us as we were then, "Not only did they have fresh ideas, they plunged headlong into executing these ideas. When it came to me, they had this implicit, unshakeable belief in whatever I said about the education aspect."

For instance, at our first meeting, Shomie had said that if we were to establish a good school, we must build an IB school. We had absolutely no idea about the IB system. But since Shomie had said it, we set about researching criteria and working to fulfil them.

Be it Shomie, Raj or I, decades after we have settled into a relationship that is today familial, our memories of that first interaction and our first idea transactions make us smile.

As a headmaster and master of so many years' standing, Shomie says he was "not bad" at sizing up people almost instantly. In his own words, "When I first met them, I sensed that Raj thrives on ideas and new things and very quickly picks up these ideas. He might not know a lot about the exact subject being talked about, but he has a sixth sense that tells him what is a good idea. NP, on the other hand, takes things, looks at them, goes deep into them and ponders on them."

There is another story that I must recount. Because it encapsulates this combination of individuals. Shomie told us that as we were starting with the early-year classes, we must have spaces that are fun for them. If we were renting a building, however small it is, we must choose a building with a tree so that the children can have a treehouse. Having said this, he never really gave it a second thought. But we looked and looked for a building with at least one tree on the grounds. And when Shomie landed up at the small building we had finally rented, there it was. A treehouse!

Our core beliefs about education were the same. While Shomie knew the vocabulary and had instituted it in his previous engagements, these same core beliefs were part of what we wanted to do with our new school. Of course, our linguistic register was not the same. The words, phrases, our vocabulary developed as we embarked on this journey. We wanted to offer child-centred education but we did not know the words.

We were like a clean slate. A tabula rasa. Whatever Shomie was writing or saying was becoming imprinted on that clean slate. As I have said earlier, we wanted something very simple – to establish a good school. We did not have any preconceived ideas or ideologies. Thus, it became so easy. We trusted him, and that was it.

But, why did I recount the story of the treehouse? Here is what Shomie says. "I laughed my head off when I saw the treehouse. But it also warmed my heart. It made me understand how much they trusted my experience and expertise. Be it building a treehouse or having women security guards in our school buses or travelling to the ends of the country to recruit teachers in order to offer our students a diverse and inclusive environment and thus create a near-perfect little world, they did whatever I asked. I recognized in them, a shared core belief system in what education should and can be. They put their faith in me, they put their own hard work and expertise with the belief that the project will work out. And it did, so magnificently, if I do say it myself!"

There is no denying that the three of us, along with a talented and dedicated team comprising Prasanna, Sitaram, Dvrk Prasad and others, have built a legacy that has defined lives. A journey set in motion at that very first meeting in Dehradun.

3

Not Another Brick in the Wall

Our journey – like all others – has been one of conversations, discussions, learnings and sharing. It is no surprise that Raj and I were in awe of this distinguished gentleman who came with such a wealth of exposure and experience. And though I wince at having to use this most overused term, the only word that somewhat sums Shomie Das up is "visionary". I will enumerate the whys.

"Has any other person apart from you ever been the Head of Doon, Mayo *and* Sanawar?" I had once asked Shomie. With a shake of the head, he had replied, "Probably not. Why? Does it matter?"

Shomie is Shomie because to him it doesn't matter that he is, in fact, the only person to have served as the principal/headmaster of the three most prestigious residential schools of India. And Shomie matters precisely because of this very same fact.

Let's get the facts out of the way first. Shomie was the principal of Mayo College (Ajmer). He then became the headmaster at Lawrence School (Sanawar) before retiring as headmaster of The Doon School (Dehradun).

His career – and largely his belief system about education – had its inception point at Gordonstoun School in Scotland. He joined Gordonstoun as an assistant master straight out of Cambridge, went on to become an assistant housemaster and finally the head of the physics department. At Gordonstoun, Shomie worked with Kurt Hahn, the world-renowned educationist known for his distinctive philosophy of school education, which is also quite clearly reflected in Shomie's own ideas.

What Shomie thinks about education can be summed up in five words – the child at the centre. And this is the first thing anyone who has seen him at work will attest to.

Wherever Shomie has taught has been centred around the comfort of the child. So many notions and perceptions we had were turned on their head once we met Shomie. For instance, I remember a fourth- or third-grader who was not only looking out of the window, but had his chair turned towards it. This, while the teacher was very much in class. I discussed this with Shomie who very firmly told me not to disturb the student. I was taken aback. Is this not indiscipline, I remember asking. Shomie had shaken his head in vehement disagreement and said, "It is not the student's fault if the teacher is so boring!"

Is this a philosophy that would only be allowed in a "new-age" school? But, even within legacy systems such as Doon or Sanawar, Shomie has always had the child firmly at the centre of his vision and execution.

Janajit Ray, the founding principal of Oakridge and a former housemaster at Doon, who has worked under Shomie at both these schools, says, "I have never seen anyone as focused on the comfort of the child as Shomie was. By this, I mean true comfort, not pampering. So seemingly effortlessly did Shomie walk the line between the comfort of the child and the rules they must respect that it was like magic to watch. He is a natural, with an instinct for getting to the heart of issues with dispassion as well as compassion. Not that students could get away with just about anything. Shomie has that aura – you know exactly when you are veering dangerously close to breaching a line with him."

Shomie always acknowledges Hahn's influence on his own philosophy of education. For some context, Hahn's educational philosophy was based on respect for adolescents who, he believed, possess an innate decency and a sense of morality but are corrupted by society as they grow older. Hahn believed that if education could provide students with opportunities for a focused growth of their personalities, for their individual leadership qualities and to see the results of their own actions, it could prevent this "corruption". In all the years that we have been associated with him, this is what we have seen Shomie do. A deep acknowledgment and respect for the child as a unique individual has underscored his life as an educator.

This is how Tushita Patel, a former student of Shomie from Sanawar, remembers him. "Shomie Das was our headmaster at Lawrence School, Sanawar, between 1982 and 1988. I was twelve years old when I joined, and eighteen when I left – too unformed to be able to analyse an adult. But what I recall strongly is that Sanawar was a safe space where I felt loved even though I was quite mediocre in most fields. It wasn't a fiercely competitive place like some other schools. Participating was more important than winning. We were encouraged to trust people, not lock our cupboards, and interact with everyone and be kind."

Tushita also recalls Shomie's and Pheroza's subtle brand of kindness. "My father passed away when I was in Class XI.

When I went back to school, I could feel both Headie and Mrs Das being extra concerned about me. But their concern was expressed subtly so that I did not feel 'special' or in any way different from the others because of the tragedy that had happened in my life. This continued till I passed out from school. But, by then, he had also made it clear that he was quite proud of how I had handled myself through it all and the person I had grown up to be. As you can understand, this is something that truly gave me a lot of strength and belief in myself. Mr Das's gentle approach towards the vulnerable students, his concern for those in need was what made Sanawar safe. A combination of subtle empathy, interest in his students and a certain kind of cool, tough love made our schooldays under his headship valuable."

This was – and is – Shomie in action. Enabling the child, empowering the child instead of laughing at them, treating them with contempt or sometimes worse, trivialization.

Ask Shomie what he thinks of sarcasm in the classroom or that all-too-common, supposedly "character-building" tool employed by teachers, especially in India – humiliation – and his usually smiling face immediately takes on a stern look, the anger just under the surface as he instantly replies, "Humiliation is no way to build character. The harm it causes is immeasurable. It completely erodes self-esteem and nothing is more character-destroying than that."

Brought up as we were on the more "old-school" ways of "teaching" a child, which quite often included not just physical chastisement but also verbal lashings, I had continued to have conversations with him about this because I wanted to understand his thought process. I remember what Shomie had said: "I know that as teachers, many of us think humiliating a child is a very good way of getting through to them. Let me tell you about a practice that existed at Sanawar when I joined. At that time, it was a regimented military school. And they used to have a practice called 'mark reading'. The whole school sat down and students' marks in exams were read out. Imagine this. A boy had to stand up, only to be told he had received 32 per cent. Imagine the sniggers. And the poor fellow. How much more can you humiliate a child? The child does not know what is happening and how to handle it. The very first time I saw this, I stopped it in the middle. There was no more mark reading at Sanawar after I joined."

I am sure generations of Sanawar students are thankful to Shomie for this!

Here's Tushita Patel again. "Before Mr Das's time, Sanawar prided itself on its military-style discipline. Mr Das came to us from Cambridge and Gordonstoun, via Mayo. He was young and I presume idealistic. His vocation was to be an educator, and his values were more liberal than what was prevalent at that time. During his time, the over-reliance on corporal punishment as a character builder eased significantly. He had a light touch, which made it easier for children who were staying away from their parents and home. Even if they didn't flourish, there was hardly anyone who saw Sanawar as a hostile place during Mr Das's headship."

"You cannot learn from a teacher you do not like," is another one of Shomie's basic beliefs about the education process. This belief has been the fulcrum of all his recruitment decisions throughout his years as an educator. This is what he would say, "The job of a teacher is an all-encompassing one because you are preparing a human being for life and enabling them to face the world. We cannot thus want only teachers who are good at academics; they must be honest and righteous individuals who teach and create good citizens. The role is extremely demanding." And let me tell you that Raj and I discovered first-hand exactly how demanding he was when it came to recruiting teachers for Oakridge.

What were his criteria? Not a M.Ed. or a B.Ed. Not a spectacular academic record. But, solid academic underpinnings, soundness of intent, interests beyond academics and, above all, a genuine concern for students.

This has constantly been demonstrated in the way he has recruited teachers. Take, for instance, Ms Purnima Dutta, who has served at Doon School for twenty-nine years. Ms Dutta says, "I first met Mr Shomie Das in 1994 as an aspiring Doon School master. It was a rather strange situation that I had landed myself in: I had very little idea of what it takes to be a teacher at the school, and even less idea of what the school was all about! However, the very nature of my extended interview was enough to convince me that if I ever got the opportunity, I would want to be nothing else but a teacher, and at no other place but at Doon, although at this point, I already had a rather exciting and promising career as a journalist. Well, I was fortunate to have the opportunity and privilege to become that master at Doon."

What was it that Shomie saw in Ms Dutta? Solid academic ability, of course, but also a spirit of inquiry, a curiosity and a love of the outdoors, underscored by an innate sense of the child as focus.

Shomie's students understood that too. As Tarun Sarwar, Mayo College alumnus and now CEO at SignAble Communications, says, "For me, what made Mr Das different was that he was interested in many different things. He used his space and position to introduce us to all of them, not as a headmaster but as an equal."

Rahul Jacob, journalist and editor, recalls the "special magic" he felt while at Mayo. "I was extremely young when my journey coincided with Shomie Das's (or Princey as we used to call him) time at Mayo. I was only seven years old and he had been principal for about a year. Even at the age of seven, I remember sensing a special magic not only in him, but also in the people he chose, and with whom he created an interesting and safe little world for his students."

Take, for instance, Captain Rohit Sen Bajaj, one of Shomie's students at Sanawar who was later to become our colleague and one of Oakridge's most distinguished principals. After leaving Doon, Captain Bajaj had studied chemistry at St Stephen's but kept in touch with Shomie and Pheroza through letters. Then, one day, he got a call from his former headmaster. "It was a telegram, actually. Come, teach chemistry at Doon, it said. I told him I would be happy to teach, Headie, but I hadn't cleared my maths subsidiary. In due course, he replied, and I remember that on 8 August 1991, I set off from Pathankot to Dehradun to teach chemistry at Doon. That started me off as a teacher, and my life's calling."

Who would Shomie consider appointing as a principal? This was a very critical subject for the three of us when we were setting up and I still remember his answer. "Well, when I appoint a principal, the two things I will look at are how well they know their subject, and what is their reputation in the classroom."

When we asked him to elaborate, Shomie said that after the principal's subject knowledge and skills level in the classroom, it was important for him to assess their willingness and ability to create a child-centred environment. "Do they really like children? Are they able and willing to make time for children or are they snowed under with administrative responsibilities? For instance, every evening at 4 o'clock when the games started at my school, I would go and stand on the field, watching children play, sometimes playing with them, then applauding them when they hit a good shot. It makes a significant difference because eventually, you will get to know all your children. I understand this is not possible today with big day schools but it can still happen in residential schools. And it is a good practice everywhere. Because, even if you cannot know all the children because of the sheer numbers, you will know more than you would if you had stayed behind your desk."

I remember clearly the firm conviction in his voice when he said, "For every principal, a child is the most important person, whoever it is – a young child, a middle-school child, a senior fellow. They are all your children, and they deserve your support. If a child is being naughty, you cannot beat them up. Sometimes, being naughty is a good thing. They are learning to take risks. If I went into a school and everyone was silent in the classrooms, I did not like it. I like the noisy and slightly chaotic atmosphere. In a child-centred space, we must consider how much involvement a principal has with children. If a principal gets stuck in their office, something is wrong. They have to be seen moving around. In fact, they have to be seen teaching."

Several students remember this particular philosophy of Shomie's with startling clarity. It seems, as soon as Shomie joined Doon as headmaster, there was an immediate transformation in the physical spaces and energy of the school. Earlier, the headmaster's office was tucked away out of sight. As soon as Shomie joined, the office became very visible – all glass walls and transparency. Everyone could see the principal going about his work.

In all schools, usually the principal is the only boss, with both academic and administrative responsibilities. At Oakridge, however, we had set up a different system. Although Raj and

I were on opposite sides of the argument on this with Shomie, we felt strongly that the administrative burden had to be separated from the academic delivery. So, we instituted the post of a director in our schools. The director's charter was to take care of everything else apart from academics and create and maintain an enabling atmosphere for the educators. Why I say this is that for Shomie, even the directors of our schools had to put children first.

Whenever we were recruiting for this post, Shomie would frame questions to help him evaluate this. For instance, he would ask candidates what effort they would put into ensuring that a child walks the least possible distance from the bus stop. For him, it was important that children did not have to walk long distances at the end of the school day. What steps would the prospective director take to ensure this did not happen under their watch?

A prime consideration for Shomie in the recruitment process was how anxious the candidates seemed about the safety of children. You will be surprised to know how safety is often not much heeded. With children running up and down the stairs, accidents are likely to happen. But this is not all. In Shomie's words, "Children's safety needs to be ensured in the classrooms as well. Children are sitting at their tables, using their chairs. These, too, can be unsafe. How? Because of the sharp corners. Often, students sit at steel tables. And these steel tables are fastened by screws that sometimes stick out. So, when a child puts their hand under the table, an accident can happen. They might cut their fingers. There are so many things one has to look after. How would the candidate approach them? That would be my question. Getting on and off buses, climbing stairs, classroom safety. Swimming pool safety. Every little thing must be taken care of to ensure safety."

It did not end there. Shomie is uncompromising on the cleanliness aspect. "Whenever I go to a school, I inspect the toilets first," he would say. "Keeping the toilets spotless, especially the ones for the older girls; these are important indicators of the principal's efficiency."

Shomie would insist that a good administrator – the principal or the director – would walk around the school and note how everything was being executed; down to how the tables and chairs were being cleaned. Nothing, he believes, is too small for an administrator's attention.

According to Shomie, "Much of the job is what you make of it. Good school administrators will be present at the school gate when the children leave for home. Just to see the children going home, say goodbye to some. This shows that the individual is interested in children's safety. This, though, cannot be laid out as the requirement of the job."

I can tell you that several candidates who interviewed with us were quite surprised at some of the questions they were asked. But all those who joined our team contributed to making Oakridge what it is today.

Another thing that must be appreciated about Shomie is that once recruited, whether a former student, or a junior colleague or senior partner, he let them be. There was always that eagle eye watching for anything that might cause hurt or harm to a child but there was no micromanagement, no overbearing supervision. This is what Capt. Bajaj says of his stint as principal of Oakridge International under Shomie's mentorship, "He would always hear me out, respond and share his perspective and not just with me. He would appreciate the person if he thought they were moving in what he thought was the right direction. If not, he would agree to have a pleasant disagreement."

Remember, this comes from an individual who was not only a former student of Shomie's but someone who had been inducted into teaching by him. What is it that Capt. Bajaj learnt about teaching from his old headmaster?

"Everything," he says. "He taught me what it means to be a tutor, to be a teacher. It was experiential learning all the way with him. He taught me that it is important to connect with children outside the classroom in order to enhance my academic delivery and make it much more effective. In terms of being a teacher, I don't give my students homework. I provoke them with questions. I learnt this from Headie. Now, the IB methodology is this – no homework but provoke a child's curiosity. But, even when I transferred to the IB system, it was not a change or a paradigm shift for me as this is what we were already attuned to, thanks to Shomie."

Another aspect that Shomie has always stressed upon is the importance of outdoor activities for children. Not only children; he got even the teachers excited. Hear it from Ms Dutta. "At my first-ever beginning-of-term staff meeting, I was surprised but thrilled that the most memorable part of the discussions was around midterms, a five-day break in the middle of the term when the masters and students went on exploratory and adventurous trips into the mountains and forests round Doon. This would happen twice a year, once during the spring term and once during autumn. There never was a single-minded focus on academic transactions within the classroom for the upcoming term. Everyone spoke and there was a general atmosphere of openness and excitement. All of us who experienced Mr Das's infectious enthusiasm and relentless encouragement consider the midterms one of the highlights of our term and a cornerstone of learning in and from the great outdoors. The midterms have always been an integral part of the Doon School education system and I learnt this from Mr Das throughout my time when he was the headmaster."

Another story that Tushita Patel tells with pride and joy talks of this aspect of Shomie as a teacher. "In Class XII, when we were sixteen or seventeen years old, Mr Das took a mixed group of boys and girls of different abilities for a trek to Chandrakhani Pass. On the day we were approaching the pass, we miscalculated and had to camp for the night just below the top. At night there was a massive snowstorm for which we were completely unprepared. We were half-buried under the snow in our flimsy tents, wet and frozen but mostly excited by the adventure we were having. The next morning we tried to trek up to the pass, but three people collapsed from pulmonary oedema and the others lost morale. We were running out of rations and our bodies were stiff from walking and the cold. Soon, we were all reduced to a pitiful mess. Headie took stock of the situation and just decided to turn back (much to our relief, I might add). There was no panic or mollycoddling and neither was there an ego issue of forcing us to continue. We trudged back through the overnight snow, quite a few of us snivelling from cold, exhaustion and fear. He led the way back without drama. When we were finally out of danger, he resorted to humour – always unfailing with young people to ease their fears. 'All our footprints have been wiped out by Tushita's bottom-prints,' he said. You see, I was too tired to walk back and chose to slide down the slopes instead, thus wiping out our footprints. This was a great experience for all of us. This was the tough love bit – no panic under pressure, no pep talks. He chose the best course of action, led from the front without letting us feel like losers. He kept it light, but didn't get involved in the smaller matters – letting us learn from the experience."

Perhaps the proof of the learnings from that unfinished trek is that thirty years later, a group of "students" from that original bunch, including Tushita, chose to do the same trek again. "This time," she said, "we managed to walk across the pass and go to the other side. We have thanked Headie for many things but mostly for inculcating in us a love for adventure, making us risk-takers who manage to have fun through it all."

As teacher, headmaster and education consultant, Shomie has played a major role in developing schools into ones that are high-quality and globally comparable. When we told Ms Dutta about this book, she sent us a beautifully written piece articulating her thoughts about Shomie. She writes, "Although one is more likely to have the fondest memories around their initial years at school, and therefore, their first headmaster, I feel that the admiration that I have for Shomie goes beyond that. And I know of many others like me who feel the same. It is when specifically asked that I realize that this is because of who Mr Das is, as an individual and as an educationist. Today, when schools across the country are speaking of the 'ideal learner profile', Mr Das lived that ideal and walked that talk since the late '80s. It was this that made the school the way it was during his time as headmaster of The Doon School: teachers and students who were always encouraged to ask questions, wanting to know more about the world around them, to be knowledgeable, open-minded, caring, principled, balanced and reflective. Mr Das himself was all of these and more, and each of his actions reflected that. I did not realize this then, I just felt deep respect and admiration, but years later, with new ideas coming into the educational landscape of Indian schools, I realized that Mr Das is somebody who is far ahead of his times, working on and implementing all of these ideals into his practice as an educationist and a leader."

As a student and teacher of history, Ms Dutta has noted the importance that Shomie has always given to inculcating in his students a sense of history while constantly moving forward. I will borrow her words again at this point. She writes, "I have always been charmed and intrigued by Shomie's unique balance of the old school thorough gentleman and the extremely forward-looking individual, a gentleman who could lead change without letting go of those facets of the past that were worth holding on to, and being carried forward."

And this has not been in India alone. For his extraordinary contribution to the development of India's top-ranked legacy boarding schools and for upgrading school education in neighbouring countries in South Asia, the Middle East and beyond, the Board of Directors and Editors of *Education World*, India's leading education magazine that has been enthusiastically supported by some of the most progressive and committed people in Indian industry and academia, such as Adi Godrej, N.R. Narayana Murthy, and Dr F.C. Kohli, among others, presented Shomie with the Education World Lifetime Achievement in Education Leadership Award in 2014 and inducted him into the Hall of Fame of Indian Education.

To borrow Ms Dutta's words again, "He never hesitated to take risks if he thought they were for the larger good and has been, and continues to be, a visionary who is grounded enough to make his vision become a reality. For all of these qualities, Shomie has been an inspirational figure for many, including me of course. Truly, I am grateful for the opportunity to have known him and to have worked with him."

But what Shomie considers his biggest achievement is that in all the schools he has been part of, he will be remembered by students and teachers alike for making learning fun, for introducing a range of co-curricular activities, for being relentlessly committed to creating a safe space and for the warmth of the relationships he nurtured.

Shomie is at the heart of what we have achieved.

4

System Error

Since that first meeting at his Clement Town home in Dehradun, Shomie and I have had innumerable conversations about education. We were building – and then running – a school together, so a lot of this was necessarily professional. But equally, one cannot be educators without vision. Given his stature, Shomie's thoughts on education in India were nothing short of a serious systems evaluation, and I am privileged to have had access to that from such close quarters.

"Curiosity is dumbed down right from Class 1 onwards." This has always been Shomie's number one concern. "Our system encourages copying and memorizing – practices that discourage original thinking. This is an extremely regressive tendency, which will keep us static," Shomie would often say.

In an interview to *The Doon School Newsletter* in 1992, Shomie had said, "Nowadays, numbers are everything. I think that whoever created our system of examination has, in fact, a lot to answer for. The dependence that our universities put on marks is very retrograde. Quite frankly, the examination system is so rote-oriented, so bookish, that I know for a fact, and from my own experience, that students who go abroad initially find it extremely difficult to work in the style the western world wants. They want an individual to think for themselves, to try and solve problems, to try and be analytical, to try and be objective, to try and research things out for themselves and not copy."

Sadly, even thirty years on, he says much the same thing. "We kill three things – curiosity, creativity and critical thinking. Children do not learn to communicate well or to make choices. These skills are neglected by our boards. Indian parents and children remain hung up on marks-as-education. Just acquiring knowledge will not help – we need to learn how to sift and use that knowledge, how to ask questions."

As a stakeholder in the Indian education system in various roles – student, parent, edupreneur – I can really find no scope to disagree with him.

Teachers are as often vilified as they are deified, but there is no denying the immense burden they struggle under. Shomie agrees. "There is great pressure on teachers to finish the syllabus and deliver marks. Teachers cannot incentivise curiosity. The natural curiosity of children becomes a punishment. In fact, children are branded as troublemakers if they ask questions. Whether the curriculum is to blame for that or the system, or whether it is our socio-cultural baggage that says children must not be disruptive, I do not know."

This forms the context of Shomie's committed advocacy of the International Baccalaureate or IB system. That's what he insisted on at our very first conversation: if we wanted to build a good school, we needed to establish an IB school. Of course, we, Raj and I, had asked why, because at that time we had no idea what IB meant!

Over the course of our years together, we came to realize the absolute logic of his belief. But as learning systems go, what are his thoughts on the merits and demerits of the Central Board of Secondary Education, the CISCE and the various state boards?

"To put things into perspective, IB does not penalize curiosity. In fact, it is an enquiry-based system. This system ensures that children have to learn to consult many sources, not just books. They have to ask and interview people, go out and see a place. So, the child learns to construct their own knowledge. And here lies the difference," Shomie would say.

Mind you, Shomie is not at all dismissive of the Indian school boards. "They conduct amazing examinations with huge numbers. Certainly, there are good schools that produce very good students. But the problem is, when these students go somewhere else, they have to unlearn certain things and relearn how to find out something by themselves. The learning system under both these boards – the ICSE and the CBSE – is bookish," he would say.

Shomie also has strong opinions about the prescriptive nature of the system, especially the fact that specific books are prescribed. He says with rare ire, "You are not guaranteed to score well in the board exams if you study thoroughly, but from a different book from the one prescribed! Because the examination is closely based on these prescribed books. Because model answers and keywords are from the prescribed book! This is where rote learning comes in. Paragraphs, long answers – everything must be memorized. Where is the place for curiosity and inquiry? The system does not empower these qualities."

Over the course of his distinguished career, Shomie has been involved with both the boards as a member. But his disenchantment with the system is clear.

Shomie's first serious concern is about the selection of books. "The way they selected the books struck me as odd. Some practices seemed geared towards helping the authors, not the students. Remember, if the board prescribes a book for three hundred thousand students, it means a lot of money for the writer," he would say.

The way question papers were set according to an unchangeable pattern also irked Shomie. He often recounts an incident that has stayed with him. "I was once asked to set an exam paper. Every year, the same question would be asked in the physics practical examination: Determine the value of g – g is acceleration due to gravity – using the apparatus. There was a pendulum. You had it swinging. You measure the time of the swing. You measure the length. Apply the length and time to the formula, and you get the value of g. I tweaked the question a bit. My question was, 'Given the value of g, make a pendulum that makes one oscillation in one second.' That question was rejected at once."

It seemed a perfectly valid, application-based question. "But my question was not acceptable," Shomie said. "I reasoned that students would use the same formula – the problem had merely been twisted a little. If a student understands the formula correctly, they should be able to solve the problem."

But that was not enough for the powers that be. "No, this question has never come before. You cannot change questions just like that," Shomie was told.

Whenever Shomie recounts this incident, he looks sad. "The boards need to produce good results. Principals want impressive results from students. The boards want to say they had 96 or X per cent success. So, this is how they achieve 'success' as they define it. Maybe things have changed a bit now."

Intrigued, I had asked Capt. Bajaj what sort of exam papers Shomie would set. My question was met with laughter. "Oh! Headie used to teach physics. He would give us open-book tests, yet we were not able to answer the questions if we had not studied. They were application-based and needed conceptual understanding. Access to the book was just not enough. He made it impossible to cheat."

And in making it impossible to cheat, Shomie fostered in his students the sense that learning was about understanding and not memorizing. As many a student would fondly recall, "How he taught us the concept of infinity! By looking up at the sky and trying to count the stars we could see."

Way back in the eighties and the nineties, Shomie was already teaching with a projector, perhaps the only one to do so. And students still remember how in 1986 at 2:00 a.m. he invited them to use his telescope and see Halley's Comet. That was the sort of teacher he is remembered as.

Coming back to the boards, I had asked Shomie for a comparative snapshot analysis of sorts. He had said, "The CISCE is a smaller board, with around 1,000 schools, compared to around 30,000 CBSE schools. The other advantage is that the ICSE has a strong English syllabus. The CBSE syllabus, on the other hand, is more pedantic. And students have to learn everything in the prescribed books."

So, where exactly does the problem lie? "It has more to do with the attitude that children need to learn from the books so that they do not learn anything wrong and so on...," he had trailed off. "People say that mathematics and the sciences are more advanced in CBSE. Perhaps it is so. I prefer the ICSE because it has a higher standard of English and the humanities, compared to the CBSE."

This is another of Shomie's defining characteristics – the unshakeable belief that a grounding in the humanities is a must for a well-rounded education and for a well-rounded human being. As recently as late 2023, Dr Ashish Banerjee, a former student of Shomie from Mayo, wrote to him saying, "You made it compulsory for science students to choose one subject from the arts. I chose history. I got 78 in history, but only 67 in physics, chemistry and biology."

This was just one of the reforms Shomie tried to introduce at the school level. With the Central government's recent declaration of eliminating the existing rigid system of "streams" in Classes XI and XII and allowing multidisciplinary choices, it seems the time for Shomie's ideas for education is finally arriving. Shomie, of course, acknowledges that, on the whole, Indian school boards provide students enough knowledge so that when they go for higher education, they have the knowledge, if not the skills.

Teaching Is Not Just Transaction

When it comes to the education system, the government is one of the biggest stakeholders. What does Shomie expect from the government, especially in light of the new National Education Policy (NEP)?

That was a question I had asked Shomie during a freewheeling conversation a few months back. Shomie had remained silent for a while, deep in thought, before coming up with a reply that only a committed educator could have. "You cannot run a school unless you are a good teacher. Teaching is a remarkably big job. The government should take the lead in producing teachers who meet the requirements of the NEP. And then ask the private sector to help in setting up teacher-training institutes."

Teaching is not just a transaction, he continued. This was, obviously, a subject he was confident talking about. "Teachers, especially in our government schools, are unaware of other needs – this needs to change. And I firmly believe that they could if they would. They are well-paid now. Government intervention is required for that last mile."

What are these other needs? I'll come back to that later. For now, let's look at what Shomie felt about government intervention.

"The government is good whenever they want to be. Look at the superb training our military and our bureaucrats get. Many of our doctors are very well-trained. Remember, most of this training comes from the government. This is why I believe the government is equipped to impart good training. It is just that they have to take the need seriously. Unfortunately, because there are no kudos attached to this profession, becoming a teacher is usually not an individual's first choice. Not to mention that teaching has largely been associated with poor pay."

One fascinating thing about Shomie is that any conversation holds the possibility of him suddenly mentioning an interaction with a significant public personality. During one of our conversations, he abruptly mentioned that he had even written to the then prime minister, Indira Gandhi, about this. And that she had actually called him for a meeting in response. So, how did that meeting go?

"That was during the Emergency," Shomie had replied. "I had written to her about the shortage of good teachers and Mrs Gandhi sent for me. But not much could be done.

Because education is not something society demands the way it demands jobs. As very little money is allocated towards education, you do not get the human resources required to impart quality education."

On another day, I had asked Shomie about his involvement in the process of formulating India's education policies? Shomie had replied with characteristic candour. "I can't say that I have had any major role. And I'm quite glad because education is in such a state that I would hate to be thought of as having had anything to do with it. Yes, I've been on several committees, but these were a waste of time. If they have used my views in their reports, to that extent, I may have had something to do with it. But I had decided long ago that I would not get involved any more in the government system."

Involvement or not, the thousands of individuals who have interacted with Shomie at some point or the other – as student or colleague, acquaintance or friend – have come away richer for that experience. Here is an incident that again shows why a good teacher is always a good teacher. Over to Jacob, who had a ringside view. "This was about a couple of years back. Princey was attending an annual cricket match between the Mayo old boys and the Doon old boys. Mayo won, and Princey, as a Dosco and a former principal/headmaster of both, said, 'Doon is the best but I am happy that Mayo has won.' This delightful sense of humour was expected. But what I remember especially is the gently insightful comment that he made, 'It's a pity that even with a match every year, never the twain shall meet…' He was talking about the fact that there was absolutely no conversation between the men from the two schools, even though this was a match that happened every single year! I remember thinking that I must do what is in my power and I made it a point to pick up conversations with some of the Doon chaps. Imagine meeting your school principal when you are well over fifty years of age, and he is still teaching you valuable lessons!" But I digress, which is so easy to do when talking about a man like Shomie.

Pastoral Care

Shomie has always unequivocally maintained that a combination of factors – the way the boards are administered, the pressure on schools for results, the pressure on teachers – converge to shrink a child's curiosity and wither their creativity. He was determined that this would not happen at Oakridge; so were Raj and I.

But learning is not all. There is the question of a child's spirit. Shomie has always been concerned about the role that pastoral care in schools played – or did not play – in the development of a child's spirit and potential as a human being.

Simply put, pastoral care is the commitment to and active demonstration of concern to ensure and empower the physical and emotional welfare of individual students, the collective student body and, by extension, the school community. Pastoral care is focused on fostering an environment and culture that supports the physical, social, intellectual, emotional and spiritual development of every student. Research findings show that pastoral care and academic outcomes are linked. This is because the physical, emotional, cognitive and social elements of a person's life cannot be treated in isolation.

Of course, Raj and I learnt the term from Shomie. I remember asking him whether Indian schools are geared to provide pastoral care. We have so many state boards, government schools, private schools and new ones mushrooming. Even in premier schools, we do not see teachers who are equipped to take care of the "other" needs of children, a point I had touched upon briefly earlier in this chapter.

Shomie's views on this are clear. He would say, "The importance of pastoral care is immense. The large numbers, along with the need to produce good results, puts state school teachers under great pressure. They don't know the children. Thus, no pastoral input is possible. It is better in private schools, but even these schools have 30–35 children on an average in a class. Undoubtedly, students are mishandled."

What about children with learning difficulties? "Teachers are not equipped to understand learning difficulties, to psychologically assess a child. They concentrate on the academically bright children. But such children are capable of learning on their own. It is the ones who need handholding that the teacher neglects!" Shomie would say.

I had pointed out that I had seen instances where teachers had informed the authorities about being unable to handle a child. "That's where the real trouble starts!" Shomie had said. "After you assess a child, how do you cope with their problems? Ideally, you have to take them out of class and give them a completely different atmosphere. Let me tell you a classic case. In the 1930s, there was this child who just could not sit still. She was always moving her hands and eyes. Today, she would have been diagnosed with Attention Deficit Hyperactive Disorder (ADHD). Her teachers told her mother to take her to a psychologist. After observing the child for a while, the doctor put on some music and asked the mother to leave the room. The doctor too left the room. When the mother looked through the observation window, she was wonderstruck to see her daughter dancing blissfully to the music. The doctor recommended that the girl should be sent to a dance school. And the mother did just that – transferred the child to a school that imparted training in dance. This is the story of Gillian Lynne, who went on to become one of the world's top choreographers. In her autobiography, she wrote that after she was transferred to this school, she found for the first time many children, who like her, needed to move around. Fortunately, she had a mother who did not force or beat her to make her conform. This is rare, as in those days beating was not at all unacceptable."

Our conversation then naturally led to what Shomie thought about corporal punishment. "Well, my mother used to beat me! I must tell you that because of the beating I learnt very well indeed! But, it cannot and should not be done any more. This is anyway much less of an issue these days as everyone knows the rules."

The issue, Shomie had continued, is that guardians and teachers are unable to detect children's problems and to give them the right inputs and stimuli. "Today, there is such a vast amount of useless knowledge pushed into children's brains. They are compelled to do things which they do not understand."

One of Shomie's pain points is how history is taught in India. "History, when taught properly, is a wonder! However, it is always taught in a dull, monotonous way. It is seen only as chronology. *When did this happen? In which year did that king die? When did that one become king?* These facts are important, but this is not and cannot be the be-all and end-all of history. If one enjoys the study of history, so many new avenues of exploration and understanding open up!"

Shomie would always say that the time constraint teachers grapple with is one of the biggest challenges they face. This is true of pastoral care even more. I remember asking him whether the government mandate for qualified psychologists in schools would be of help. "Yes, of course," he replied. "But this is a mandate of the private boards; I don't know about government schools."

In fact, one of the reasons for Shomie's preference for residential schools is that teachers – and often their families too – can give a child more time and individual attention. I remember a conversation where he had said something very poignant: "We must not forget that school can often be a refuge for some children." How simply he had put it! Yes, schools, especially residential schools, can to an extent balance out difficult situations at home.

"Many of my teachers were very good counsellors and children would naturally gravitate towards them," Shomie had continued after a pause, recalling names from his vast archive of memory. "Take, for instance, Amarnath Dar at Doon; his house was always full of children. The way he fought for his students was remarkable. I remember that I once remarked at a staff meeting that a particular student was hopeless and needed to face consequences. But this man kept on fighting with me, doggedly. Other teachers would have backed off much earlier, but this man would never let a child down. I used to keep goading the teachers because I wanted them to think about the effects of pulling the rug out from under a child. At Dar's house, you would always find at least one child being fed an omelette by his wife. Quite often it would be past the mandated bedtime and, if found out, the master could have faced consequences too. But our masters understood that, sometimes, giving children the opportunity to talk things out was better than enforcing the rules. This is the sort of teacher the system needs."

Needless to say, Shomie himself was precisely that kind of teacher. Totally involved. So invested he was in his students' well-being that he had no problem recognizing them and remembering their names decades later. Jacob, Shomie's former student I mentioned earlier, recalled a meeting with his former Princey years after he had left Mayo. "I met him at a friend's house after about thirty years. He didn't hesitate for a second, greeting me with, 'How are you, Rahul? How are George and Jonathan?', referring to my two brothers! We have remained in touch since then. He also knew exactly what I was up to regarding my work. He asked pertinent questions that couldn't have come from an uninterested person. I remember I had written to him when I got my first job and they, Princey and Pheroza Ma'am, had sent a card. He never ever missed responding to someone who had reached out."

Back in his days as a teacher, that quality of reaching out manifested itself in his focus on making education more child-centred. He reached out to the child, irrespective of their individual merit, with zero tolerance for teachers who brought in their own biases and prejudices. "Teachers," he would say, "must remember to treat all students the same way and yet be attuned to their individual needs, talents and personalities."

No wonder then that Shomie is one of those rare teachers his students are privileged to call their friend later in life. Capt. Bajaj remembers wistfully, "When I graduated, Mrs and Mr Das gave me a cologne which I kept for two to three decades; it was so precious. Later on, I was privileged to call them friends. I remember Mrs Das serving us cold soup, roast chicken and mashed potatoes. Again, easy effortless elegance was always a hallmark of theirs."

Before I end this chapter, a few words on the teaching profession itself and its skewed gender ratio, a topic I deal with in greater detail in the next chapter. Shomie would often talk about the dearth of good teachers coming into the teaching pool straightaway. Again, it's the effect of the system where the focus on engineering and other professional career paths has made teaching an almost last-chance career choice. "Low pay levels mean a teacher's income cannot be the primary one, making teaching itself a second choice. With women's incomes still being the second in the family, teaching thus becomes a preferred profession for more women. In a country like India, being taught by only or even mostly one gender creates new issues and exacerbates existing ones," he would say.

But Shomie is an optimistic man. While his decades as an educator have given him a unique clarity on the issues the education system faces, he has never allowed these to be a barrier to doing his best for all the students on his watch. For Shomie, it has always been "Onward and forward!"

5

System Reset

What we have seen in the previous chapter is that the problems that ail the education system in India are clear and many. The solutions? Definitely not clear and very definitely not many. The primary problem that has been identified by most educators, though, is the sheer number of students and, hence, the pressure on teachers. Shomie too acknowledges the pressure on teaching staff but feels that more can definitely be done.

In India, he says, teacher training is nothing more than transacting a subject in a classroom. "Yes, an imaginative teacher does all they can to make a class interesting. But look at what is taught in the B.Ed. course? A lot of theories. How is that going to help a teacher?"

Teachers, Shomie believes, need to learn how to interact with children. "There are so many skills one needs to learn. And these cannot be taught in a B.Ed. college. I, for one, never studied B.Ed. You can learn these skills only through actual classroom teaching."

Having been a part of the education sector, I have come to agree with what Shomie says. Of course, B.Ed. courses do have classroom teaching but the main focus is on theories and what they call lesson plans.

"Do you think teacher training should be done away with?" I had asked Shomie. It was another of those freewheeling conversations we regularly had, our germination pool of ideas, as we used to call them. Shomie's reply was not what I had expected. "Not at all!" he had said. "In fact, I believe that students should be taught to be teachers right after they finish their Class XII, not after graduation. That is, those who are interested in taking up teaching as a profession. A four-year degree in teaching would produce a stream of good teachers. Then, you can get a multiplier effect."

Shomie has always felt that the government should take the lead in producing teachers, especially now in the context of the NEP, and then seek the help of the private sector in setting up teacher-training institutes.

"How would that work?" I asked him. His answer was emphatic. "I have long thought that what certainly is required is a cadre of dedicated soldiers in education, individuals who are committed to teaching in the true sense of the word. And I wish we had a cadre as large as the Indian army. The army preserves the integrity of our country. I feel that another way of preserving the integrity of our country is to have a cadre of teachers of uniform quality who would be committed to imparting holistic education to children."

Shomie's point is simple: with good teachers, one does not even need a school building, because good teachers, he feels, can teach even under a tree if need be.

This is what Capt. Bajaj says. "One of the most significant things that Shomie taught me was the importance of teacher training. Teacher training at the individual school level, not qualifications. You must remember that while IB doesn't require academic credentials such as B.Ed. and M.Ed., CBSE requires them, and compliance must be achieved. But he was never happy with just that. He demonstrated how to connect with teachers, not just communicate. It was wonderful how much he encouraged all around him."

But then, probably the main problem the system faces is that teaching is almost never a first choice as a profession. Shomie had agreed and sounded almost wistful. "Yes, unfortunately education does not attract the very best as it should. I wish I could attract young people to teaching the way they are attracted to engineering, medicine, banking or even the services. If education could attract people like that, we would, within a very short space of time, perhaps even in one generation, improve the quality of life in India. This is where the government needs to step in."

With what, I had asked.

"Policies that enable the creation of good teachers," he replied.

Now you know why Shomie has constantly iterated the need for an educational service. "If teachers are produced like we produce our officers in the services, it will attach prestige to the profession," he would say. "Pay and perks will follow. Only then will the best even consider teaching an option. Today, because of low pay scales, or what in economics is called pay-scale distortion, teaching is mostly left to women, because a woman's income is still largely the second income in a family. It is important to make teaching an option that anyone can consider as a primary or single source of income as well."

A Balance of Genders

According to data, in the private sector, more than two-thirds of all teachers are women. This imbalance is most visible in elementary and middle schools.

Is that a bad thing, is the next logical question. It's not bad, but it's not ideal either, Shomie says. He believes that teaching, like anything else, needs a balance of the sexes because children need to see professions as gender-neutral in order to make the world more equitable. And, in any case, he feels, any balanced situation requires the presence and involvement of both sexes.

This is why he battled to recruit women teachers when he helmed Doon and was responsible for getting the first women teachers into the grand old school. "In my co-ed schools, in Sanawar, for instance, I had men and women of equal numbers. But in Doon, there were mostly men, till I started taking women as teachers. Now, there are quite a few women teachers. You need to have both sexes. They bring different perspectives to the table."

Coming back to salaries, Shomie has always fought against pay-scale distortion in his engagements as a school administrator. He himself had been a sufferer in his early days as a teacher, even in Gordonstoun. He was paid £300 for the entire year, that too on a half-yearly basis. He would receive £150 on the first of January and another £150 on the first of June. Of course, teachers there would be given free board and lodging but that was only for eight months in a year, when the school was open. They had to fend for themselves for the remaining four months, and it was not easy.

Fortunately, Shomie had a good bank manager, a family friend who, he said, allowed him a certain amount of overdraft. "Those days, bank statements were handwritten. If you had money in the bank, they used black ink. No money, red ink." That is where the idiom "in the red" comes from, Shomie had explained, ever the teacher.

"Well, the bank manager must have been a very nice man," I had interrupted, smiling. "Oh, yes," Shomie replied, refusing to take the bait. "One day, he wrote to me, saying, 'Dear Mr Das, you really must look at the colour of the ink on your statement. It makes all the difference between poverty and riches.' That was a particularly good advice, but I could not do anything about it. You cannot live that kind of a penury-stricken existence."

In fact, the reason for his separation from Mayo was the school's refusal to pay the teachers what Shomie thought was the basic minimum. "When I transferred to Mayo, some senior teachers were being paid only Rs 250. I had come with a huge salary, a whopping Rs 2,000. And my vice-principal, Mr Danval Mathur, was not getting even half that amount. He had been in the school for close to half a century. I took that matter up. But I left Mayo because I could not convince the board."

Rahul Jacob recounted an incident that occurred in relation to Shomie's exit from Mayo, and which speaks of the lifelong impact Shomie has had on building character. It seems that when the students at Mayo came to know about his resignation, the senior batch went on a strike of sorts. But what was truly lovely is that Shomie called them in and instead of expressing gratitude, he insisted that their parents were paying the school for their studies, not for them to indulge in strikes. "There was absolutely no spite in him. It was remarkable that even in leaving, he taught all of us such a valuable lesson."

Coming back to the question of pay, teachers at Doon had been getting pretty much the same salary for over twenty years – about Rs 8,000 a month before Shomie joined. But Shomie kept fighting for pay parity and by the time he retired, senior teachers were earning close to a lakh, which was very good for those times.

As an entrepreneur myself, my question to Shomie has always been how entrepreneurs or the public sector can help with this. What does the education sector need from entrepreneurs? As part of the partnership that built Oakridge, we have lived this process of need and supply. We have done our best to establish a near-ideal school where Shomie could bring all his ideas to fruition.

The Economics of Education

It is always interesting to look back on our conversations about this. Also, having run three residential schools of the scale of Mayo, Sanawar and Doon, Shomie understands the economics of the sector all too well. He recognizes that entrepreneurs need projects with the possibility of cash inflow. But he has a legitimate concern, which he expressed very well.

"From my personal experience, I am afraid a lot of entrepreneurs run schools solely to earn money. And the whole sector gets a bad name. It is imperative to make a profit, for the simple reason that without money an institution cannot function smoothly. One has to maintain the infrastructure, pay salaries to staff, and so on and so forth. But, in educational entrepreneurship, money cannot and must not be everything."

I agree completely. Both Raj and I were conscious about this with Oakridge. We did our best to balance child-centred education and business imperatives. We believed that business imperatives were necessary for the benefit of students. Schools have to run business-wise, or else they cannot survive, staff and teachers cannot be paid. Without money, one cannot upgrade facilities or create a conducive environment to facilitate learning.

Ask Shomie about the way business was handled at Oakridge, and this is what he will say: "NP and Raj were conscious of the fact that teachers had to be paid well. And that was one of the things that got them into trouble. They had to borrow money and take big loans. But they could not charge a higher fee."

What necessitates charging high fees? First, of course, is the capital cost of building the school. When establishing a new school, one cannot spread that cost over seven or eight years. One has to add classrooms and improve facilities all together.

So, one constant balancing act that was caused by Shomie's mandate – and our acceptance of that mandate – was finding a good teacher–student ratio which we maintained at 1:10. We fixed the class size at twenty-five, plus two children of staff members in each class and this ratio was strictly maintained. Yet, when you need money, you need students. The more the number of students packed in a class, the greater the money earned. This is always a conflict for which there is no straightforward solution.

Then, we had to pay teachers who taught dance, painting, swimming, sports and other activities. Students had to take part in these activities but, from the exam point of view, these are secondary. So, again, what's the solution?

Actually, there isn't any clear-cut solution. As for Shomie, questions such as these are the conflicts entrepreneurs face and have to handle. The optimal balance will lie in the intent.

The Ideal of IB

As far as learning systems go, Shomie sees the IB as the ideal. He feels that the system is attentive to the quality of teaching. Under the IB system, teacher-trainers are sent to schools to ensure that, and he thinks that the government also needs to follow this. The ICSE and CBSE boards do conduct similar workshops and teacher development programmes but he feels they have to be more broad-based and on a bigger scale.

"IB is not about knowledge that is handed down by the teachers and the system. This is what I mean by an enquiry-based learning system. IB is more of a facilitator for life skills and attributes like resilience, curiosity, and lifelong learning. And this makes IB the differentiator."

To sum up, then, Shomie believes that a good school needs to pay its teachers well and provide a conducive atmosphere for learning. And a good teacher cannot just be good academically – they must be honest and righteous individuals who teach and create good citizens. The job of a teacher is an all-encompassing one because what they are essentially doing is preparing a child for life so that the child is ready to face the world. Needless to say, it's a demanding role.

6

Beyond the Blackboard

A teacher's job, then, is demanding.

But how demanding? That's something only those who are involved with education would know. One reason is the pressure of sheer numbers in India – the millions and millions of students who enrol every year. That makes finishing the syllabus, more often than not rushing through the mountain of texts, the be-all and end-all of education delivery.

As someone who has been associated with education for nearly three decades now, I can hardly deny that. That's exactly what is happening. The result is, the holistic development of children and, by extension, generations, gets tossed out of the window.

"Children need much more from us – as educators and as primary architects of society," Shomie told me once. But the reality is that the vast majority of teachers, especially in our government schools, are unaware of what children need. This is again where the government needs to step in.

"What would you have done if you were given the authority?" I asked Shomie.

"I would have ensured that teachers in the government sector were properly trained and sensitized. If they are properly trained, I am sure they would become the most willing and powerful agents of change."

What Shomie primarily wants is for teachers to "see" children as individuals with individual needs. Remember, children spend a big part of their waking hours in school. A major concern in recent years has been the lack of services and resources for the psychological well-being of children. While the Government of India has successfully implemented several initiatives to ensure enrolment of children in schools, a push on similar lines is required to address their mental health in school environments. Across the board, qualified psychologists are required in schools.

Both the central boards have mandated that all schools must have psychologists on their rolls. The IB system has, of course, always had this requirement.

"But why is it important to have psychologists on the rolls?" somebody had asked Shomie. We had just launched one of our Oakridge campuses and had called over some friends to celebrate the occasion.

"Bullying and other acts of violence can harm a child, not just physically but emotionally too," Shomie explained. "Psychologists in school can identify and help at-risk students, aspects where the school is vulnerable or lacks awareness and prevention programmes. But till schools manage to comply, the burden of care remains on us teachers. And we have to be equipped and willing as much as possible to handle such matters."

In fact, one of the reasons for Shomie's preference for residential schools is that teachers, and often their families as well, can give a child more time and individual attention.

Let me cite an example. It seems a gentleman, who has been one of Oakridge's most distinguished principals, was a bit of a loner when he was a student at Sanawar. It's a story I have heard from an unimpeachable source. Shomie himself.

"He was lonely in the sense that he did not make a lot of friends. He was actually not a very 'boy's boy', so to speak, and so was often left out. But Pheroza was very fond of him. And he would spend hours with her. But this boy was not just a sensitive boy. He was brave too and decided to push his own limits and step out of his comfort zone. After finishing his bachelor's at St Stephen's, he went on to join the army, where he did a Short Service Commission. That is because he realized that he needed to go through a process that would test his manliness. This interesting fellow, Captain Rohit Sen Bajaj, went on to become a teacher and a very good one at that! He has taught at Doon and at Sanawar, before taking over as the principal at Oakridge."

As mentioned before, Capt. Bajaj has been a significant member of the Oakridge family. Both Raj and I have seen Capt. Bajaj at work and he has always come across as someone in command of all situations. That's why this anecdote is so illustrative of the effect pastoral care can have on an individual's growth and trajectory.

This is what Capt. Bajaj says about Shomie outside of the classroom. "We were allowed to go to the Das's home at any time whatsoever. It might be exam time or just to play with the many doggies they had. We were served coffee and toast in fine bone china on a wooden tray. The style and class with which they approached their everyday life really inspired me.

I used to dream that one day I would live like them. In their style, and by style I do not mean anything to do with wealth but everything to do with elegance of the mind. He, and they, were inspirational."

Jacob agrees. "Pheroza and Princey held a kind of open house and pupils could walk in and out of the principal's house with impunity. They were so much fun to be around informally, that even as a very young child, the sense of magic was clear."

Encompassing Differences

Coming from an individual who was himself a "different" student, this insight is invaluable. Teachers must be made aware that differences exist, and that it is okay for differences to exist. Often, a teacher walks into a classroom and expects thirty to forty children to absorb or respond to the same lesson or task in the same way. But learning cannot happen this way. Children's minds might draw a blank. They will keep questioning why they are doing what they are doing. Most of these things become meaningless to them. Shomie's point is, it becomes difficult if teachers are not trained. And the only way he could train teachers was by doing it himself and showing them how education delivery could be child-centred.

To put it in a nutshell, he believes that if teachers learn to recognize, acknowledge, appreciate and work according to differences, they will encompass all differences. This by itself is sensitization training.

Talking of Capt. Bajaj leads Shomie to remember with fondness his own teacher, Jack Gibson. "You know, I was so proud when Sir rang me up in Scotland and said that he wanted me to take over from him. Can you imagine what a moment that was! My teacher telling me that he wants me to take over what he is leaving. Remember, teachers can get through to everyone if they try. And they must! When I became the principal of Mayo College, I was around thirty-three. The principal lived in a huge house with fourteen bedrooms. When I arrived there, Gibson introduced me to his staff. One of them I recognized immediately. He was the *maali* when I studied at Doon. The gardener too recognized me. Gibson was surprised and asked him how he knew me. 'Sir, he used to steal carrots from your garden at Doon,' the man replied. Gibson immediately recalled that I used to do that and laughingly told me that he had to give me a 'putt' (a little smack on the bottom) and we had a bit of a laugh!"

Before joining Mayo, Shomie had learnt a lot from Kurt Hahn when he was at Gordonstoun. Hahn's philosophy would have a significant influence on Shomie's outlook on education. Hahn had identified two pillars of education – character-building and a sense of honour entwined with a sense of obligation. There was a third pillar too. Trust.

What I have gathered from Shomie over the years is that Hahn meant children to understand that one is always a member of a community and that, attached to this membership, is a sense of obligation. It is clear that this approach profoundly influenced Shomie's. It became clearer when we had conversations with his old associates at the legacy schools. Janajit Ray, for instance, Oakridge's founding principal, would often talk about Shomie's commitment to fostering a sense of community service.

As would Capt. Bajaj. "Community service was another pillar Shomie was committed to as a teacher. I was there when the Uttarkashi earthquake happened and he mobilized us to help in the rescue and relief efforts. From him I learnt that social service is an essential part of who you are and that it shapes how we look at and treat others. Especially those who have not been born into privilege."

One thing I learnt from Shomie that was quite at odds with my idea of Doon, as only for the children of the elite, was that every year Doon took in ten students on government scholarships and government bursaries. As students and teachers have both asserted, Shomie ensured that the students who came on these scholarships and grants were treated with respect and with the awareness that they had brought in an element of diversity that was important for the other students at the school. Some students remember that Shomie studied the demographics of the school and found out that most of the students were coming from a 200-kilometre radius catchment area. He then started the system of conducting intake interviews across the country – in Kolkata, Mumbai and other cities across India.

Frankly speaking, none of this had come up in our conversations with Shomie because the CAS programme – creativity, activity and service – are built into the IB curriculum and requirements. IB students have to do some service as part of their curriculum. But when Shomie recounted how he had devised programmes based on the Gordonstoun model that integrated a sense of community service with outdoor activities and a tolerance for risk, I was fascinated.

"How exactly do you teach, or inculcate, trust and honour?" I had asked Shomie.

"By actually implementing them at a personal level," Shomie responded.

"And what does that entail in practice?"

Shomie thought for a few moments, then replied, "Well, you tell a boy that you did not approve of something he has done. Now you want him to do something as a consequence and a task is assigned. This task would be unsupervised. No one else would even know that this amounted to a punishment. But the student would have to later report whether he had done what he had been tasked to do. There was always the chance that they might lie but, remember, children generally don't like to lie. This has worked very well for me. Another way of inculcating trust and honour is giving senior students lots of responsibilities. They did what was good for themselves and the school, thus keeping themselves on the straight and narrow. Of course, this is not as straightforward as it seems because children sometimes did wrong things and needed direction."

Interestingly, two of the examples Shomie always gives involves vehicles. It seems he used to drive an Austrian vehicle called Haflinger, a fascinating light utility vehicle, around the 300-acre Mayo College campus. The boys, of course, were quite envious. One night, Shomie recalled, with a twinkle in his eyes, he heard the car start and drive off. "I ran downstairs. I knew they would have to come back the same way since the path was circular and stood there. When they came back, I stopped them. I had a tennis racquet with me and whacked a boy on his bottom. The strings broke. I told him he would have to pay for the restringing. Till date, I get a Christmas card that says, from 'the boy on whose back you broke your racquet'! But what is really interesting is what happened the morning after. I had called the boys to my office. They anticipated trouble but turned up. One of them gathered the courage to ask, 'Sir, may I say something?' When I gave him permission, he said, 'Sir, my father used to be in school with you. He said that you did the same thing when you were in school.' The fellow was right, because I had stolen my headmaster's car the same way. So, I looked at him and said, 'Yes, I did, but I did not get caught.' This is one of the things I thoroughly enjoyed – getting the boys to take risks. It was not a great, immoral thing. Just a naughty prank here, a little mischief there. It is necessary to take risks in life, and I admire this quality. One needs to weigh the pros and cons of the risk."

Shomie can recount many similar instances because breaking bounds is a part of growing up and all teachers have their share of such stories. What is rare is his candid admission that, as an educator, he secretly felt this was a good way of teaching children to take risks, to weigh up their risks, to predict what might happen if they are caught and, in the process, learn to be more realistic.

Out of the Classroom

Another way of encouraging holistic development is to take children out of the classroom as much as possible. That's vital, Shomie says, to building physical and physiological strengths and also primes children for a life of activity.

This again brings us back to Hahn who thought risk-taking was a crucial element in character-building. Hahn was responsible for setting up a landmark initiative: Gordonstoun for Rescue Services. Since the school was by the sea and close to the mountains too, there was a coast guard service and a mountain rescue service as well. There was also a fire service team.

"Hahn thought that you must teach children to rescue lives," Shomie would often say. "He felt that was equivalent to fighting for your country in times of war. He always believed that one has to learn to be alert, to see if someone is in difficulty and to go and help them. Students were trained for fire service, in mountain climbing and rescuing. And mind you, they were part of the adult service, not an isolated little group of children. The fire brigade was part of the Elgin Fire Service and if there was a fire, they would be called and suddenly three or four boys from a class would get up and run out. Hahn trained children to be good citizens."

Shomie tried his best to implement some of these thoughts at Doon since he too believed these were important for character-building. He even set up an ambulance service. In those days, ambulances were hard to find. When an earthquake struck Uttarkashi in 1991, they drove the ambulance and carried out rescue work in villages, pulled people out from under piles of debris and took them to hospitals.

But the service was eventually discontinued. "Today, these things are considered a waste of time. Principals are under pressure to get the best academic results. Character-building takes a back seat," Shomie rues.

He would often talk about another incident, which happened while he was at Gordonstoun. Shomie had taken fourteen boys to climb a peak called Ben Alder. They had camped at the bottom of the peak for the night and set out the next morning. As they climbed, a severe blizzard started. The wind was strong and the blizzard froze their eyelids, which meant they were climbing without being able to see where they were going. On their right was a sheer slope.

"All we had," Shomie recalled, "was a map and a compass. Then this boy said, 'Sir, let's put the map on the ground and align it.' In the strong blizzard, we managed to do that. We aligned the compass and walked ten paces. Then we did it again, another ten paces. Finally, this boy led all of us to safety. The interesting thing was that, in class, he was a very dull sort of fellow. But his real character came out in this tough situation." Shomie calls this a universal phenomenon.

Later, while he was at Mayo, he would lead another rescue effort during a flood. Shomie had received a call from the district collector who asked if they had boats. "We did. So, off I went with ten boys and one master in our boats. We did a lot of rescue work, helping people perched on trees, taking them home, feeding them and giving them shelter. Among the boys was a fellow called Anil, who sadly is no more. He was very naughty but I had deliberately chosen him. The master had strongly advised me not to take him but he turned out to be the best in the whole group. He volunteered for everything difficult. There was hardly any drinking water. So, Anil would walk a couple of kilometres, often at night, through flooded areas to fetch drinking water. His character came through in that crisis."

Shomie is an incurable optimist. And if there's something I have learnt from him, it is this. There is no point being an educator without believing in the potential of our children, our future.

7

A Legend and a Legacy

It was this shared belief and a commitment to the future that first brought Shomie, Raj and I together and has since kept us in the same frame over the decades. But what did this association mean in real terms? Simply put, a school and then a group of schools that would come to represent as ideal a learning environment as possible in India.

"Let's call it Oakridge," I remember Shomie suddenly saying one evening when we three were driving around Hyderabad. Raj and I had agreed immediately. That is how Oakridge came to be named. An off-the-cuff statement followed by immediate acceptance.

We agreed without any question or even any discussion. But I do remember asking him how he had so quickly arrived at the name that was not only catchy but also distinctive.

"A neon sign which said 'Oak Wood' just caught my eye," Shomie had replied. "And that transported me back to when I had applied to the Oak Ridge National Laboratory in the US for a job as a scientist. I had not been selected for the job. So, why not name the school after this world-renowned research centre?"

So, what exactly has this school named Oakridge achieved to be called a legacy?

A simple Google search will tell you that Oakridge International is not one school but a group of five, spread across Hyderabad, Bengaluru, Visakhapatnam and Mohali. But then, there are many such groups of schools and simply being part of a big group does not extend any legacy status.

Just a little more research will make it clear that Oakridge's education delivery record across parameters for both the International Baccalaureate Diploma Program (IBDP) and the International General Certificate of Secondary Education (IGCSE) has been superlative. Oakridge has an established history of excellent academic outcomes, with students achieving world-level examination results and going on to secure places at the best Indian and foreign universities.

But it is not only the numbers. Oakridge students – whether they are in Class I now or are university students – can be identified by their confidence. Not of the arrogant variety but a confidence that stems from a fair evaluation of one's own capabilities and self-belief. This is ensured by Oakridge's focus on dance, music, theatre, community service and models and events such as MUNs and Hackathons, among others. This is Oakridge's biggest identifier and differentiator, and I am sure the students who have passed through its gates would wholeheartedly agree with me.

The Child at the Centre

That's a strong joint legacy but how did we create it, given the different backgrounds that Shomie, Raj and I come from, our different personalities and the diverse experiences we have been through?

It was like two forces coming together. Shomie agrees with this. He always says, "NP and Raj accepted that the principles, the mechanisms of education delivery at Oakridge should simply be what I thought it should be. There was never any conflict about this."

What are these principles? As I have written before, what Shomie thinks about education can be summed up in five words: the child at the centre. Raj and I agreed with his views and worked hard to implement this at Oakridge. Everything at Oakridge was designed around the child. For the comfort of the child.

There's another aspect to this. For a teacher in the classroom, there may be twenty-five students. Sometimes the teacher doesn't even know all the names. Students are referred to as "left bench", "back bench", "red-colour shirt". This is what hundreds of students are reduced to. But that "red-colour shirt" is somebody's life. Can you deal with someone's life that way? Can you reduce them to anonymity? As a teacher, you have been assigned the responsibility of nurturing a child. If you treat a child as just a roll number, it is dehumanizing. It takes away the student's identity and individuality.

At Oakridge, education revolves around the child. But at that time we did not think of this as "child centred". It was Shomie who called it 'child-centred education'. He would say that what we simply called a good school meant a child-centred school. As I have said before, our linguistic register was not the same. The words, phrases, in fact the entire vocabulary developed as we embarked on this journey together.

Still, this does not explain what made Oakridge an institution, different from the schools offering five-star facilities mushrooming across the country.

Bear in mind that there can be many motivations for people to establish a school. One is to make more money. Then there are the well-meaning few who establish schools because they feel the existing system is faltering. They have new ideas; so why not implement them? But one point needs to be factored in. Other than an educator, everyone else has to depend on one or many persons when starting a school. But who can be considered an educator? Creating an institution isn't child's play. Some people write a cheque and they expect institutions to be created with just that cheque. We must remember that many headmasters or principals are successful in schools that have already established a reputation. They may not know what it takes to build an institution.

Also remember, neither the educator nor the founder is aware of the existing gap. Through this lens, we must question how many successful businesspersons are becoming educators. The answer, of course, is not many. While they may have the intention, they do not have the time. What then often happens is that these huge buildings, these edifices, end up lacking a soul.

One reason for that is what I just highlighted. Some promoters bring in a principal with a good reputation and start getting numbers. But numbers and money cannot sustain in the long run what a school's essential objective is. What I mean is that, this should not be a profit-seeking business only. This is about institution building and the process of building an institution requires a radically different approach from building yet another business. Some businesses may eventually become institutions. But most businesses remain restricted to being businesses, and never become institutions.

At Oakridge, the three of us built a business that also happened to become profitable and hence financially sustainable. Were we aware of this difference when we started out? Of course not. To begin with, there was no explicit awareness that we would venture into institution building. This clarity has evolved. Even the very difference between business and institution is an insightful observation that we fine-tuned over the years.

What we did was ask ourselves certain questions, beginning with what is an institution? By definition, an institution is meant to outlive us. Even businesses last beyond a lifetime. However, institutions are created with a bigger purpose, one much larger than a financial motive. While working on the Oakridge schools, we realized that every school was an extension of society, with its students and their families, and the teachers all components of that society. A school exists within a society and so, it must truly serve that society. It should have all the traits of that society and be an extension of that society. And it must serve a transformative purpose. This is what we consider an institution.

Let me elaborate. Once, I was speaking to an engineering team and I realized that the building we were constructing was going to outlive us – we must approach construction with this mindset. The specifications, the designs, and the construction as a whole must sustain themselves. Similarly, all the policies that go into making an institution must be thought through. We have to consider it this way: if I'm not there tomorrow, how will others see it? What will be their response? Have my personal biases shaped a policy, or is it relevant and significant? Have I been able to popularize my policy and implement it consistently? In most cases, a policy is written with one intention, but different people interpret and apply it differently.

Operating from misconceptions and errors in implementation are as good as having no policy. Because I am there in a chair, I assume the power to interpret things the way I find convenient. But not all things are meant to suit one's imperatives. What will happen is that when I won't be there tomorrow, another team will come up with a different interpretation. When that happens we would be straying from the real meaning of the policy.

So, having a coherent policy framework with a purpose is another important characteristic of institution building. Until headmasters or principals are encouraged to approach institution building with this mindset, the buildings shall remain massive campuses without souls.

Quality and Diversity

Shomie's instructions were never to compromise on the quality of teachers and the exposure we offered to our students. When the board wanted us to have expatriates as principals on the reasoning that they would bring in a new culture and add to the diversity quotient, we agreed, but I remember Raj emphasizing and Shomie agreeing that perhaps no other country had such indigenous diversity as India.

We got down to the all-important job of recruiting the best teachers. For this, we had a simple formula. Love for their subject and love for children. We felt that everything else can be taken care of, can be inculcated through training, can be worked out and also worked with. But it was only when love for the subject and love for children converged that a teacher could bring joy to their classroom. Only then can a teacher develop in students not just interest but a fascination with lifelong learning. Not that this joy always translates into a love for that particular subject that the teacher is teaching but the children understand the sweetness of the process of learning and the self-directed rewards of curiosity as they delve into subjects that attract them and, sometimes, even those that don't attract them that much. And that is very important.

As always, our model has been Shomie. Let me tell you that Shomie has had a lifelong passion – that of radio telescope research. His fascination started in college and he continued his exploration at Gordonstoun, at Mayo and at Sanawar – for over twenty-four years, he explored one subject! That is love for one's chosen subject. So, every time he was teaching students, he was undoubtedly transmitting this sense of excitement and fascination with learning. Let me tell you another story that illustrates this. When the first wave of COVID-19 isolated us from each other, I had one day called to check on Shomie.

"NP," he said, "I am very busy these days. I go to bed at around 2 a.m. You see, there were some topics that weren't explained to my satisfaction when I was in college and now I have discovered the most fascinating YouTube videos explaining those very well. I am relearning those topics." Can you imagine? Eighty years plus and such interest in his subject! This was the standard we aspired to offering our students while recruiting teachers for Oakridge.

Shomie was always keen on ensuring diversity. And he acknowledges that Raj and I were open to it too. "It was fortunate that both of you understood the value of this," he would tell us.

To others he would say, while recalling our journey together, "NP and Raj actually went to Calcutta and Assam to recruit new teachers. When I said we should have teachers from all over, they went all the way up there to that end. I told them to focus on teachers from Bengal as they almost always have some extra skills such as painting, dancing or singing. If not themselves skilled, they had an understanding and appreciation of the arts and definitely a wider worldview." In fact, our first principal was Janajit Ray, who had come from a journalistic background and had also served at Doon.

Both of us, Raj and I, feel that this diversity was one of the key factors behind the success of Oakridge, and should we start something similar in the future, we would surely replicate this model.

People Plus

But it was not enough to simply get the best. It was also important to retain the best in order to become the best and remain the best. Towards this end, Raj and I set up robust people policies that eventually led to Oakridge being ranked among the Top 100 workplaces in India for the four years that we participated, with the highest being 15 in 2019, the last year of our association with Oakridge. But, numbers aside, we can with utmost sincerity say that we tried more than our best to take care of our teachers and staff.

But all that required a lot of effort, self-belief and commitment to an ideal. What was this ideal? It was, quite simply, the value system that Raj and I shared as a result of our similar upbringing.

For instance, back in 1993 when we had just started Vikas at Visakhapatnam with a lot of effort and were beginning to get enrolments, we had a young tutor who was mesmerizing in the classroom. An engaging teacher, he quickly became very popular among the students and through word of mouth we started getting more enrolments. A few months later, we heard that a questionable intimacy had developed between him and a student. We were in a dilemma. If we let him go, we were sure that it would be catastrophic for our numbers at that early point in our journey. But if we stayed silent and let him stay, it would set a bad precedent. The whole night Raj and I discussed this and, in the end, we both agreed that no matter what the consequences were, this was unacceptable to us. If someone was in a position of responsibility, their conduct should not only be unimpeachable but also unquestionable. We asked the teacher nothing but told him to leave. This decision did not have the negative consequences we had feared; in fact, over the years, more and more students joined. Our uncompromising response led to an unwritten rule that everyone was aware of: if ever any male teacher's intent or behaviour made any female employee or student uncomfortable, it would lead to an immediate parting of ways with us. No written complaint, no investigation would be required.

We had made our stand clear and since then, in all the institutions we founded and managed, we rarely had to deal with similar issues again. So, twenty-five years after that incident, when a working women's organization came up with a list of best places to work for women, we were in the Top 10. And mind you, the Top 10 were not ranked. No, we had not set out to win awards or a place in the rankings. We did what our hearts prompted us to do.

The Love Quotient

Raj calls it the love quotient. While I may not use such an emotional term for it, the love quotient has played a huge role in our success with people. Simply put, our belief – again shared – is that in all our interactions, the love quotient should not only be a strong driver but one of the most important factors.

Again, this was not a deliberate strategy or tactic. What we did came naturally to us. Step into the shoes of the other person and your conduct immediately becomes regulated.

Twenty-four years ago, we had instituted a system of feedback for teachers at Vikas. Since this was a preparatory junior college for students of Classes XI and XII, we thought they were mature enough to process and express their feedback. We came up with a self-assessment tool as well. This questionnaire had thirteen questions and the requirement was it had to be filled in by all the teachers. They did not need to show it, but had to fill it within a given time period. Once the student feedback was received, we would share it with the teachers in the strictest confidentiality. Then, they themselves had to analyse if their assessment was aligned with the feedback. "Please let us know only if there is a serious concern or misalignment," we told the teachers. Usually, there wasn't much misalignment. The students were always more generous and forgiving than the teachers themselves.

Everywhere, we managed to establish an environment of trust. We were not a very high-paying organization but even when there was competition, with others offering double the salary, our people were not willing to leave. Let me rephrase that – money was never the incentive that could make people leave. Of course there were separations but they happened because the opportunities were better or different or more challenging – never simply because the money was more. That's the true measure of our people policies – that they found the organization supportive.

When we started participating in the *Economic Times'* Great Places to Work Awards from the year 2015 onwards, after more than twenty years of running institutions, we ranked 105 across sectors. There was no separate section for education and while we were more or less happy, we wanted to earn a place in the Top 100. The very next year, they started a separate education category and we ranked No. 1. Across sectors, too, we kept getting better and better till, in 2019, right before we exited, we were placed Number 15 overall. Mind you, this had the Tatas, ITC, Microsoft and Mahindra – all the big corporates. Still, across sectors, we ranked 15. Objectively speaking, this was a phenomenal achievement. But again, looking back, we never did what we did keeping rankings and awards in mind. Whatever we did, we did because it seemed right to us.

One external testament to this came when the team from Nord Anglia Education came to Oakridge during the exit process. The CEO, Andrew Fitzmaurice, said, "We have more than sixty-one schools across over thirty countries all over the world under our umbrella but nowhere have we seen such happy faces as at Oakridge. What is it that you do differently?"

Well, we do not know what the faces in other schools look like; we simply know that we tried our best every day to ensure that there was no dissatisfaction or discontent.

Given the scale of the enterprise we were running, we had about 300 buses and that many drivers and conductors. Over 600 support staff were part of our workforce. Though trade unionism is quite rampant in the regions in which we operated, we never faced a single day's unrest. Not a single day did transport get hampered. As any school will tell you, that is a huge thing to have managed.

I will also speak about an insight that we gained over these years. Wherever the salary is higher than the market standard, unionism will take hold. The reason is simple – expenses rise along with higher income. Thus, if employees are unhappy for any reason, they will not leave but want their environment to change. So they stay, build a narrative, rally people around them and soon there's trouble brewing.

Managing the Manager

There is a truism – people join the organization but leave the manager. To ensure that this did not happen at Oakridge, we put robust systems in place. We must remember that managers are not often able to handle all the people they manage. Interestingly, when it comes to discussing appraisals and performance reviews, managers often tell those who directly report to them that they are meeting the expected standards or even exceeding them. But when it comes to writing the appraisal, they have complaints. So, there is a disconnect. The employee never gets to know that they need to do better in order to meet expectations and the organization too loses out in terms of improved performance. Unsupportive managers are difficult to work with, both for the individual and the organization.

So, we put in place a system under which, every fifteen days, managers had to enter scores on specific parameters from a given drop-down for every individual reporting to them. Even "no specific observations" was given as one of the options. This forced the manager to report any issue within fifteen days of it first appearing and eliminated the possibility of concerns coming to our notice five or six months after it had occurred or, sometimes, even one appraisal cycle later!

Also, once this was entered into the system, it was visible to the employee as well so that they could also take corrective action at their end, if needed. If the employee was in disagreement with the observation, there was a system to record that as well and to escalate it to the next level for evaluation of whether the particular professional relationship was functional or profitable to the individuals concerned and the organization.

The Parent Thesis

Although parental satisfaction is a part of customer satisfaction and does not fall under people policies per se, at Oakridge, we believed that as the primary stakeholders, parents were very much our people and their satisfaction and comfort were our responsibility.

As an edupreneur with so many years of experience, let me tell you that there will always be disgruntled parents for a variety of reasons – both valid and not-so-valid. But never was there any situation we could not handle. Let me cite an instance. In Mohali, we bought out an existing school that the previous promoters had run for three to four years. To the parents of existing students we said we would continue the old fee structure but for new students, there would be a new fee structure.

Some parents then organized an agitation of sorts across two days – there was sloganeering, blockades when the other students were entering the school, and so on and so forth. We immediately sent a senior executive from Hyderabad to support the principal and the staff. Everyone was given very clear instructions – water, tea, coffee and food must be sent out at regular intervals to the protesters. They were agitating, yes, but they were the parents of our own students and distressed at that point. True, we did not agree with their chosen means of expression, but they were neither our enemies, nor outsiders, but important stakeholders, and we were their service providers.

I had also made a practice of holding meetings with parents. We had asked our class teachers to identify the most unhappy and disgruntled parents in each section. This made up a total of about forty in all and I invited them to meet me along with the principal and the coordinators. Only twenty turned up. Of them, only about ten voiced their concerns. Second, our approach was clear: we had not arranged these sessions to apportion blame or even to explain ourselves but simply to identify shortcomings. But more often than not, the simple act of being heard was enough to assure them that their concerns would be taken care of.

The 'H' Factor

If you ask people why they were happy at Oakridge, they might not be able to articulate it perfectly as it was always a combination of factors and never a single one. For instance, Capt. Bajaj might tell you that we threw a reception at the school when he got married and that he doesn't know of many employers who would do that. For us, it was but natural.

All in all, those who worked with us over the years simply knew that they were happy and this was clearly visible to all who visited us. The high "H" factor was probably a combination and convergence of intent and intuition. All we can say is that it was happiness all around.

The Business of Utopia

According to Raj, any educator at one level believes in utopian ideas. "Without being utopian, they cannot be effective teachers," he would say.

But to be a successful businessperson, they also need to know what it takes to create a sustainable business. When they don't know how to do it but think they do, a situation of crisis is born.

Between the three of us, we not only averted crises but made crises work. And the formula that worked seems to have been this: identifying the heart of the institution – the principal. That was the first step. The next steps were to enable the educator by being profitable, by being sustainable, getting the best resources, and ensuring that the institution pays for itself over and beyond. So that the institution could continue to grow and serve.

But, again, we could not have created this with just any other educator, however able. Shomie is an institution unto himself, a legend, for more than one reason. Every person he has met and influenced along the way – and let me tell you there are many – will vouch for that, maybe even mention newer aspects of his character that makes him who he is.

It's our privilege to have been associated with him for more than two decades now. That also probably makes Raj and I uniquely placed to talk about the legend that is Shomie Das and the legacy we jointly built.

8

The Trust Quotient

Just as we are uniquely placed to talk about Shomie, so is Shomie uniquely placed to talk about us. By us I mean Raj and I, and of course the journey the three of us started together. In fact, it was Shomie's excited response that set me thinking after I had come up with the idea of writing this tribute to him.

"But I want to talk about you two as well!" he had exclaimed. "How you gave me a playground and a 'karmakshetra' for all my dreams and vision about education. And I want to talk about our journey together!"

It was then that I realized that this book could also be a memoir of our journey, which has taken on a powerful organic life of its own.

It's not that we always agreed on everything. A key point of difference was the role of the principal. This difference in opinion still persists but that has never affected our relationship. Nor has it in any way impacted Oakridge. But I'll come back to that later. For now, I'll plunge straight into what Shomie thinks about us.

To put it in his own words, "Tweedledum and Tweedledee!" Trust Shomie to come up with that, but that's a compliment, as far as he is concerned. "NP and Raj are like Tweedledum and Tweedledee! NP spends hours on details. The spaces to optimize learning from and things like that! We need that," I remember him telling someone.

"Raj, on the other hand, had no time for this. He would be off in a corner talking to somebody, trying to understand their issues. This is what makes us a good team. One of the things about both NP and Raj is that they are willing to listen. They were never reluctant to accept new ideas."

How much Shomie appreciates us has always been a point of quiet pride for both Raj and me. We all brought different strengths to the table. For instance, if you ask Shomie about Raj, the first thing he would say is that Raj is an incredible asset to have when it comes to people, whether they are teachers or parents. "He is an interesting man. When I first met him, I thought, 'What is this man going to do?' But it turned out that I was completely wrong. The way he presents and teaches is incredible. He understands with great clarity the kind of issues teachers face. And he addresses those impeccably. While he was not a classroom teacher, he is incredibly good at directing teachers. Now, who knows how that works? But it does!"

Again, a cumulative retelling of Shomie's understanding of us is this: "Raj and NP are both highly intelligent but in different ways. NP will explore the philosophy of a question and then proceed. As for Raj, he is a problem solver. You give him a problem, he will take a look at it and commit himself to solving it. In every area. When we started the school, Raj had the task of getting 500 kids for the school. We had just lost around 180.

But he went ahead and did it. In fact, he got a hundred more than 500. He has this knack of taking up challenges and has the intelligence to solve them."

I remember overhearing a conversation between Shomie and someone else. Shomie had been asked how much of the entrepreneurial journey he was privy to or had been burdened with.

"It is not easy funding an educator's dreams and vision," he had replied with startling clarity. "But they kept their commitment. They did indicate to me the problems and some of the struggles they faced, but when I told them that struggle would be an integral part of what they had set out to do, they believed me and carried on."

We understand struggle, Raj and I, and the value of money, too. Let me tell you about an incident from my childhood. My father used to involve my brother, Sitaram, and me in the operations side of his overall responsibilities in running his school. He would give us a specified amount of money and send us to Vijayawada to buy certain things. He would give us Rs 10 for the commute, nothing extra. That meant we had to think twice before we could have a cool drink, which probably cost 50 paise in those days. There was no cushion. But because we were young and, like all boys of our age, susceptible to such innocent temptations, we would spend half a rupee on a cool drink. As a trade-off, we would carry the luggage and walk back instead of taking a bus, so that we remained within the budget. That has taught us many lessons, including investment and cash management.

Shomie understood that we were worth his time and trust. Actually, he understood us individually and collectively as a team. "Raj is someone who thrives on ideas and new things and very quickly picks up these ideas. He might not know a lot about the topic being discussed, but he has a sixth sense that tells him this might be a good idea," he would often say.

"NP, on the other hand, takes things, looks at them, goes deep into them and ponders them. They are both very understanding but different from each other. One is very much into the details of how to do something. The other is a man of ideas. But what we have together is something intangible. It is what we have inside, the people we are and the combination we built. Together as a group, we put our faith in each other and our hard work and expertise into the project. With the firm belief that it will work out. And it did, magnificently."

Shomie would also praise our networking skills. "Both Raj and NP are particularly good at this. They network well. They are constantly talking to senior bureaucrats, to politicians and holding meetings. They understand it is crucial for them to do so to build a great institution," he would say.

He would appreciate our sense of connect with the milieu, too. "Hyderabad attracts people from abroad as it is a hub of software companies, from Microsoft to Accenture. And NP and Raj understood these people."

The Conflict

Coming back to our disagreement on the role of the principal, Shomie feels that the principal is the person who represents a school and should be the one to deal with all the stakeholders. Both Raj and I, especially me, had a different perspective. I felt that in a school of 3,000 students, multiple aspects had to be taken care of. Some of these must be left to someone of equal importance, rather than have the principal shoulder all the responsibilities. So, we appointed a director who formed a link between the school and the management.

Shomie feels the way he does because he himself has had a lot of administrative experience in his capacity as principal and headmaster at Mayo, Sanawar and Doon. "I was not only in charge of the students but also finance and maintenance and even the staff," Shomie would say. "There would be a host of issues, such as ego tussles among the staff or children fighting each other. All came to me. When a Group 4 staff got married, I was asked to be the officiating high priest. And I enjoyed this role because I really 'knew' everyone."

I had once likened all that to being the commanding officer of a battalion. "Yes and no!" Shomie had replied. "A commanding officer has several assistants. But I did not. We were left to ourselves."

That had given me the opportunity to edge my theory in sideways, i.e., getting a director on board. If you look around you will see that in most big schools, principals look after the academic side and an administrative manager looks after the other side. That is, again, because of the numbers. A total of 3,000 students would mean 5,000 parents. We have to set up systems. The first point of contact for a parent is the class teacher and I agree that if it's a serious issue concerning a child, they would eventually want to consult the principal. But the director should take care of everything else.

A question we were often asked when we started this system was about the boundaries between the principal and the director that must not be breached. Sometimes, the tone of the questions would become a little aggressive because, as promoters, we were thought to be primarily concerned about making money.

Despite our differences, Shomie always stood up for the system we had in place. "At Oakridge, the boundaries are very clear," he would say. "The director takes care of all the administrative responsibilities, but no decision about the school that concerns students or parents would be made by the director. The principal would be in charge of this side of things."

That's one of the boundaries we worked out. While we never questioned his suggestions on the academic side of things – Shomie has always acknowledged that – this separation of responsibilities was necessary. For one, we felt that principals – and educators in general – were in some ways out of touch with the imperatives of the real world.

For instance, we had an expat principal by the name of Gustav Gropp who, on a particular Sports Day, asked the chief minister's wife, daughter and daughter-in-law to leave a shaded area in the stadium as that was not a designated area for families! He was not wrong but, at the same time, this is not something you can do in India.

As Raj would always say, "Educators remain somewhat divorced from the world outside. They often do not realize we live in an imperfect world. We have made the world inside the school walls near perfect. But that is not the scenario outside."

Shomie, however, never had this disconnect. He would even recount his experiences to the teachers in a bid to instil a sense of real-world practicalities. If you live in a world like India, he would say, you have to be aware of the society you are living in and your surroundings. "I had to move my boys in Mayo College four times a year by train to their homes and bring them back. For that, we required railway ticket reservations. One needs help from the railways. I always cultivated relationships with the parents who were in the railways. Because, that is how the world works. If the district commissioner came and told me that someone needs admission, I would obviously ask them to send the student and I would see what I could do. There are always people one needs to depend on to run a school, especially a boarding school. The principal has a leading role in seeing that the school is well thought of. And this does not happen only with good results. It has to be built in different ways so that people say, 'Oh, Oakridge. That's a great school!'"

Hundreds of Components

Running a school involves hundreds of components that require thorough knowledge of the diverse aspects of sustaining an institution, such as operations, marketing, management, project capacity, and a whole lot of other things. While Shomie is an educator par excellence, we did not depend on him for these. Raj and I, with our other colleagues, handled these aspects. We brought our knowledge, our understanding and our networks and relationships to the table. Our experience with Vikas, the junior residential college we established in Visakhapatnam, also helped us.

But all this – taking care of the logistics, including nutrition, hygiene, staff-related matters and transport services – is an enormous task and we didn't want to put any additional burden on the principal. That's why we decided to hire a director to take care of these operations. The principals were not always happy with this setup as they had been part of systems where they had to take care of all such things.

But as long as we were involved, we did it our own way, combining our diverse skill sets, respecting boundaries and never letting our differences supersede the wider objective of turning Oakridge into a world-class educational institution. And that is what we have managed to do by enabling an educator, by being profitable, sustainable, getting the best resources, and by ensuring that our joint endeavour pays for itself over and beyond.

9

Ten on Ten

If we are to summarize the principles or commandments by which Shomie has lived his years as a visionary educator, and we have learnt to live by, this will take the form of what Shomie calls "The Ten Cs". Even today, "The Ten Cs" hang on a wall in his study, for ready reference.

These principles or commandments are basically ten key traits or aspects that Shomie believes need to be nurtured for both personal and collective well-being, irrespective of whether one is a student, teacher or parent, or simply someone interested in the question of human beings achieving their full potential.

So, here they are, in order.

1. Curiosity – The faculty of being curious is at the root of all knowledge.
2. Creativity – It is creativity that underscores our unique individualities.
3. Critical thinking – The ability to analyse, evaluate and solve problems is critical to human growth.

4. Choice – Learning how to make the correct choice among the plethora on offer is often indicative of a person's success.
5. Communication – Communication lies at the heart of our interactions as a social entity.
6. Candidness and courage – Honesty and sincerity and thus courage, form the bedrock of communication.
7. Collaboration – Along with communication, collaboration lies at the heart of successful human enterprise.
8. Competition – The need to better oneself every single day stems from the natural sense of healthy competition.
9. Citizenship – As citizens of our communities, nations and the global collective, living the responsibilities and rights of good citizenship is a must.
10. Compassion – And above all is compassion, the ability to truly 'see' the other, and a faculty that empowers appropriate choices.

It was with our individual and collective commitment to "The Ten Cs" that Oakridge as an institution could continue to grow and serve. This has been our story, a narrative of trust, collaboration and mutual respect. In the next section, I will take you through the stories behind this story.

Section II

Our Stories

10

The Making

What you have read so far in this book is an account of a journey of education as an enterprise but one where the roadmap was a bit different from what we usually see. We have already dealt extensively with that in the preceding chapters, so there's no point in going into it again. But that's just one aspect of the story. The story would be incomplete without what went into making that story. In other words, how it began.

But my apologies! Let me reintroduce myself first. I am Tummala Naga Prasad, the author of this book that you have been reading and, well, the protagonist of my entrepreneurial dreams. Fortunately, some of those dreams have come true, through a combination of factors as we have seen.

Anyway, to get back to what I was saying, this is an account of that beginning. Of how two small-town boys, who grew up in a semi-rural environment and studied in schools where teachers merely taught but never inspired, established an institution like Oakridge, a school whose primary objective was to not only ensure a deep grounding in education but to also free the mind to explore beyond the constraints of curriculum. It was tough, very tough, because the odds were stacked against us. The main reason was lack of money. Establishing a school requires money, for acquiring land, for constructing the building and the basic infrastructure, for hiring good teachers, and for sundry other things. But we didn't give up, driven by our desire, lurching from one loan to another, yet never losing sight of the summit – our goal of building an institution that would set the benchmark for others.

Looking back, it seems like an adventure, but one that tested all our resolve and character. It helped that Yarlagadda Rajasekhar, or Raj, my childhood friend who has been with me through this long journey, and I shared the same passion and similar values.

Then, somewhere along the way, we came across Shomie Das, our greatest mentor in this enterprise of education. But I'll return to him later. For now, I'll go back briefly to where it all started, a farm where cattle grazed in open fields and the afternoon haze was a blur of brown and indeterminate green.

We, Raj and I, are from Nuzvid town in Krishna district in what was then undivided Andhra Pradesh. The town's economy consisted mostly of middle to lower-middle-class people, who were content doing what they did best: live from one day to another. Both of us were from middle-class landowning families that had other means of livelihood too. While Raj's father, Nagamuneswara Rao, was a government agricultural officer, my father, Venkateswara Rao, had started a school where most of the children were first-generation students. The seeds of our future enterprise were probably sown there. Raj and I would study together in my father's school from Class II to Class V.

Diverse Exposure

While growing up, I would help tend the buffaloes and the cows, doing all that was required of children born in a farm. I would go and fetch grass for the milch animals and, in the sowing season, I would water the plants. When it was time to harvest, my brother and I would help pluck vegetables. These days going to a farm means relaxation; back then it was actual physical labour. It was hands-on exposure we got and we lived that experience, imbibing common sense along the way. That kind of exposure, apart from being diverse, also kept us grounded and down to earth. Looking back, that was a key trait we picked up then – that of simple, modest living – and which probably saw us through later during those difficult years as cash-starved entrepreneurs when a frugal lifestyle was the only way we could survive. Those were early lessons that we learnt as children.

When I look at children now the first thing that strikes is how different our childhood was. Also, how different our parents were. Unlike my parents, who I hardly remember asking about my exam scores, most parents today, I realize, see the child's performance through the prism of how they themselves had fared as students and make it a personal thing. As a result, the pressure on children now is way too much. We were lucky. Whether it was by design or by default, we were given a diversity of exposure, with no pressure of academic performance.

That, of course, didn't mean we had unbridled freedom. Whatever we did, we were expected to do with responsibility. There was, however, a flip side to the diverse exposure that we got. We could not concentrate on academics as we grew up. It didn't also help that there were no inspiring teachers at the government Zilla Parishad High School where Raj and I studied together again from Class VIII before pursuing different streams; he engineering, I mathematics. The teachers were good people but they never wowed us. I never had that kind of opportunity of meeting inspirational teachers till I had completed my post-graduation.

A teacher, I believe, plays a big role in the life of a student. If you ask me, teachers should not only be a source of knowledge, they should also inspire the children to see merit in learning and get the children to be actually learning. Their role should not be limited to dispensing classroom lectures and assessing academic performance; it has to be that of a facilitator. We tried to implement that in Oakridge and have, I believe, succeeded to a great extent.

Meeting of Minds

The man who made that possible is Shomie. He is a scientist at heart, never averse to experimenting with ideas to bring about changes within the system. All his ideas were focused on how to make the lives of students more interesting and how to make them curious, an approach that perfectly gelled with our own vision. In a way, Shomie was the inspirational teacher we lacked in our childhood. Oakridge, then, was really a meeting of minds, one willing, the other able.

This section is largely an account of the prelude to that meeting of minds, of how seemingly unrelated circumstances would one day fuse into one common narrative; basically, the story behind the story, as I mentioned earlier in this chapter. It's a thread that straddles two progressions, separated by time and distance. Shomie, if you recall, was born thirty years before us, so his journey started much earlier than ours. It would be a circuitous journey, across continents, but we were destined to meet. It was sheer providence that we met but that's how fate works.

For the convenience of readers, this section alternates between our story and Shomie's; one an autobiographical narrative that begins in Nuzvid and at times goes back and forth; the other a biographical account of Shomie's life. It is a narrative that unfolds like two parallel tracks but with a difference – because the tracks eventually meet.

11

A School Called Home

Peter Pan. Long John Silver and his chattering parrot. Gulliver in the island of Lilliput. Tales from Tagore in Bengali. This was after-dinner routine, every day.

Half an hour of stories by his mother while he would be tucked into bed. By the time he drifted off to sleep, he would already be away, flying with the boy who never grows up. The mornings, though, would start on a more serious note. Learning to read and write; spellings and grammar, both English and Bengali. Additions, subtractions; long divisions. All that in three hours of study. Not a minute more.

After that it would be time for lunch. And no study for the rest of the day.

Every story, every idea has a beginning. And while one does get to sometimes choose where to begin from, the seeds may have already been planted. For Shomie Das, it was at home where it all began. That's what I would gather from the extensive and often freewheeling conversations we had.

Despite the difference in years, we would interact more like friends. I would call him Shomie, he called me NP.

Shomie was home-taught before he went to a regular school because his mother, who had been educated abroad, didn't like the way kids were taught in school, especially the rote-based memory system that was used. His home-schooling would last only a few years but it would shape his future as an educator, someone who instinctively knew what could help children learn better.

Years later, after Oakridge had become the school of our dreams, Shomie would recall his childhood as he and I one day sat in my office talking about how our early learning influences our way of thinking. "You know, NP," he said, "I was home-schooled from the age of five years before I went for regular schooling. My mother was concerned about the way children were being taught. I am talking about 1940 or thereabouts. Once I had been sent to a school in Burdwan when I was staying with my grandparents but it wasn't a happy experience. The teaching in class consisted of looking at scrawls on the blackboard, copying from the board and memorizing. We all did our homework by memorizing the lessons. Sums were done on the blackboard and then we simply did them all over again."

So his mother had taken on the responsibility. "My mother taught us how to read, write, add, subtract, do long divisions, LCM and HCF. And, of course, tables; we had to learn tables right up to sixteen. And that is how we spent three hours in the morning after breakfast. My mother would give me exercises to do sitting next to me. She was quite strict and if I forgot spellings it used to be quite severe. So I tried not to forget spellings. Grammar is something else that we were taught very well, both English and Bengali grammar."

Guava Tree and Bedtime Tales

But it was never all work and no play for Shomie and his sister, Reyhaan Das, who was a year older. His mother, an accomplished and formidable lady, though strict, would give the kids free time to play. After lunch they were completely free. They lived in a house with a beautiful big orchard with guava and mango trees, among many other kinds of trees. It had a deep well, full of water. "It used to be fascinating sitting under a guava tree, munching on guavas, chatting with all the friends I had made there," Shomie would recall. I had a sudden vision of a boy climbing a guava tree and making a mess of the clothes he was wearing.

"Tell me, Shomie, were you an obedient kid or a naughty kid?" I asked him.

Shomie had laughed. "Trust you to ask that question, NP, but yes, I was quite naughty and would get beaten quite a lot. My mother used the brush on my bottom often." Then he suddenly became serious. "But I am grateful to the way she taught me and gave me the fundamentals so thoroughly. She used different techniques, including storytelling. Every evening, she would read a story to me. They were from old English classics, like J.M. Barrie's *Peter Pan*, R.L. Stevenson's *Treasure Island* or Jonathan Swift's *Gulliver's Travels*, and also tales from Rabindranath Tagore and Sukumar Roy in Bengali. This was a daily routine. We were given half an hour of stories by my mother while we were being tucked into bed. That was one of those very nice ways that we learnt. It was never thrust down our throats. The point about home-schooling is that you are in familiar surroundings and learning was comfortable, not full of the uncertainties you face in a classroom. I was also curious about what my sister was learning. She was one year older to me and so ahead in the books we were being taught from."

Shomie is now in his late eighties but clearly remembers those early days. Years later they would play a big part in his becoming a teacher with a vision. Needless to say, much of the credit for that goes to his mother, Sujata Das.

"My mother was very advanced and accomplished. She got a degree in English from Edinburgh University. She was educated well in the western ways and she used that knowledge when she taught us. She taught us Bengali, English and arithmetic."

It was fascinating to hear him. Of course, it was a privileged upbringing that included cars, ayahs and personalized attention, but to Shomie's credit, affluence was never a distraction. Shomie spoke about his father, Dhruba Ranjan Das, too. "Our father had sent us away from Calcutta to Ranchi because of the war (World War II). When he came to see us in Ranchi (in modern-day Jharkhand) for holidays, he would stay with us for two or three days. Father had an easy-chair. I would sit on his side and he would talk to me about things in general, like what was going on; who was fighting whom; how our car worked, breaking down complex things into simple information that a child could process."

A Story Out of a Situation

Ranchi, then in Bihar, had its own charms. "There were a lot of military people in Ranchi and because of that one of the games we played was to form an army. We would go marching up and down with sticks as our guns. So, that was the kind of learning that took place, and we learnt to make a story out of a situation. Our imagination would run wild and that is what my mother wanted; to use our imagination."

When he was a little older, Shomie would follow the reports that appeared in the newspapers and be fascinated by the grainy black-and-white pictures from the war front. He supported the Allied forces because the Indian Army was involved and there were soldiers everywhere in Ranchi as a reminder.

"You know, NP," he told me one day, "I remember the day the Germans surrendered. I got a Union Jack and went around with it. Then I hung it from my house. A few months later America dropped the atom bomb; I was awestruck. Japan surrendered a few days later. That was called V-J Day, or Victory over Japan Day. I got another flag. This time, my flag had King George and the Queen. Not that I was a great supporter of the British royals, but the flag was the symbol that good won over evil. That is the kind of feeling that I had."

Another person, Shomie says, who taught him a lot was his maternal grandfather, Dr S.K. Sen. He was a doctor and Shomie used to be sent away to Burdwan where he worked as a senior medical officer to the Maharaja of the then zamindari estate. Every morning he would sit and shave and have his tea at the same time, all the while talking to Shomie and the other kids and teaching them basic science through practical demonstrations. For instance, he would pick up the kettle of hot water he used for shaving and pour some water on the ground. He would then ask why the water was moving in the way it was, encouraging the children to think.

Then there was Hemangini, Shomie's ayah (attendant). She would tell him fascinating stories. Each story had to do with tigers and honey gatherers, big rivers, crocodiles and a deity called Bonbibi. Shomie had visited the Sunderbans a few years ago and all those tiger and crocodile stories he had heard would come alive. It was then that he realized that Hemangini was from that area.

Hemangini was a widow who lived with Shomie's family as a paid employee tasked with taking care of the children. But to the young boy growing up away from school, she was a window to a different world. A fascinating world of fierce, wild animals and a life as exotic as it was perilous.

If he could, would he trade any of that, I asked him. Shomie had smiled and replied, "I was fortunate that I did not have to go to school and was allowed a free run compared to most others my age."

To Shomie, home-schooling is a continuous process. "It is like sitting and eating together," he would say. "Mother would be talking, Father would be talking. He would talk about the day. They had arguments, while I would be fed up listening to them. But you learnt lots of values. Everything else you can learn if you go to school. But it was values that my parents taught me."

This was something I could also relate to. Back in Nuzvid, my parents too had taught me the basic values of honest hard work and prudence. Later on, that would help me keep my feet firmly on the ground. How a child learns to adjust also depends upon their upbringing. A school is a place where children spend a limited amount of time. Out of the 365 days in a year, a school works for only 190 days. And of those working days, it is only six hours at school. If you look at it that way the overall time spent by a child in school is a very small percentage of their life.

Of course, school is an essential part of a child's growing-up years but it is the parents who have to form the personality of the child. The society the child is part of also has a lot of influence on how they grow up.

Transmission of Values

"What was home-schooling like?" I asked Shomie one day.

He thought for a while before replying. "My mother was very keen to see that we picked up knowledge, values and so on. She would write and read to us. Today, which mother has that kind of time?"

If one really thinks about it, Shomie continued, before schools were invented, it was all home-schooling. "Parents passed on their knowledge to their children, like the trading classes would pass on their craft and their skills. Children would also learn just by observing their parents. It sounds like a new concept today in this age of smartphones, which have brought information to the fingertips for everyone. Apparently, you don't need to have a parent to teach. The point I am trying to make is that if parents can spend time with their children, there is an interesting transmission of values. It was a simple thing. What they found funny, I found funny. That may not be so for someone else. I remember my mother trying to be spiritual, but she just wasn't; and even I tried but just couldn't be. Spirituality never attracted me. But my great-grandmother from my mother's side, whom we used to call Boroma, was spiritual by nature. She would go to the Ganga every morning. Being a widow, she wore a white sari. She was also a very orthodox lady and if I touched her while she was eating, she would stop eating and go and bathe again. It was fascinating to watch my great-grandmother and it was through her that I was introduced to the Bengali culture. I must tell you that in her young days, my mother was a consummate actor – she went dancing in the evenings but pretended never to. But I digress!"

That was typical Shomie, polite and ever the gentleman. He thought he was digressing. I found it fascinating, the musings of a man whose memories had recreated themselves as a template for what early learning should be like. A template that had been nurtured at home.

Shomie gathered his thoughts. And he seemed to have anticipated my next question too. "I really don't know if home-schooling was popular among the elite in those days. I think our parents were compelled to home-school us because families were sent away to mofussil areas because of the fear of aerial bombing by the Japanese. I remember the first time the Japanese came in, the frightening sound of fighter aircraft zooming in, the wail of sirens, anti-aircraft guns shooting and then searchlights crisscrossing the night sky. The next day we learnt that the Howrah bridge had been bombed. So my father sent us away."

Peter Pan and fighter planes. Long John Silver; a strange world of fierce tigers and a fabled guardian spirit of the forests. Afternoons in the orchard, the bitter-sweet tingle of green guavas on the palate. Shomie's childhood was like a series of picture-perfect frames, carefree save for the three hours of language, grammar and elementary mathematics every morning. The walls of a classroom were yet to fully intrude into his life as everyday routine.

Till how long should a child be home-schooled?

"I support home-schooling up to a certain point," he replied. "Basically, parents must help the child learn script and writing but not take part in full learning. And second, they must always interact in a way that brings discipline. The whole thing is discipline."

Shomie's first taste of discipline would be learnt at his mother's knee; remember the "brush on his bottom"? The disciplinary "strokes on the bottom" would come later, but not at home. That would be at Doon School, which he would join when he was ten years old.

But we would leave Shomie with his reminiscences for the moment and return to him as a school-going boy in another chapter. For now, it's time again to revisit a small town in Andhra Pradesh.

12

Concept to Creation

The 1980s was drawing to a close, hurtling towards a new order after a momentous decade that saw the Berlin Wall crumble and the emergence of new computer technologies. India too was evolving, with a law that granted eighteen-year-olds the right to vote becoming one of the symbols of change. But some things don't change – one of them being the allure of the civil services.

From ambitious urban youths to those in the rural hinterland, the pull of the bureaucracy with its accompanying privileges that come with power and status unites all, irrespective of background. To be honest, I was no exception. For a while this fascination would draw me into the race. I had even joined a coaching centre, like thousands of others, all of us young graduates enamoured of the promise of success these institutes offered.

Some people might say it's a case of sour grapes – I'll leave that to my readers to draw their own conclusions – but what I experienced left me disappointed. There were hardly any good teachers and most of those who took classes at these centres dictated from old notes compiled over the years. In a way that also reflected the general attitude to study. All that mattered was how to crack the test so many would sit for; learning was secondary.

So I pulled out from this race. It was not for me. Then one day, while talking about my experiences with my friend Prasanna who still dreamt of joining the country's elite bureaucracy, the idea struck. Why not start an education centre, perhaps a junior college? And, if we did start one, how different would the institute be from the others? I later discussed the idea with Raj. That was the genesis of Vikas and, eventually, Oakridge.

But wait, we are getting ahead of the story. Let's rewind a bit. To the time when Raj and I were still small-town boys in Nuzvid, on the cusp of adulthood. It's a story full of twists and turns, rambling in places, at times even seemingly irrelevant to the main plot, but then life hardly travels in a straight line. It's also a story rich in memory, with deeply personal tributes and full of little lessons valuable enough not to be forgotten.

A Unique Teacher

Raj and I went to the same tuition master when we were in the tenth grade. Vishnu Sharma was a unique person. In those days he would tuck his shirt in and look very dapper. And because he was different from the others, we would make fun of him. Behind his back, of course. But he could be strict too. He would take only twenty students from the tenth grade and cherry-pick those he wanted in his tuition class. The two of us were among the twenty he selected though we had no intention of joining the tutorial sessions. The daughter of our school headmistress also studied in the same school but Vishnu sir refused to admit her to his tuition class. He told her that twenty students had already been selected and that was the limit. And, no, he wasn't going to budge. Period.

I have later on mentioned this in many of my talks when referring to Oakridge. In the very first year of starting Oakridge, we got a request to admit the then education minister's grandson. If the boy was to be admitted, it would have had to be over and above the limit of twenty-five students we had set for each class. We stuck to the rule and refused him a seat. I am proud to say that we never broke a rule at Oakridge. There was pressure, from politicians and other influential people, but we never violated this rule and that was our guiding compass.

Coming back to Vishnu Sharma, one of his colleagues once asked him, 'You are a respected teacher. But everybody makes fun of you. Still, you have always remained cheerful. How could you be like that?' The tuition master replied, 'Look, once you are prepared to accept garlands, you have to be prepared for the stones too.' Vishnu Sharma lived in Hyderabad for the last years of his life as a bedridden invalid till he passed away. Raj and I used to visit him occasionally till his last days.

The first time we went, we were visiting him after a long gap of twenty years. There was no way the lady of the house could recognize us but because she knew we were coming she came to the door and addressed us by our names. When we asked how life was, she said, 'Your sir is bedridden with old age; I am old, so I am bent, but God is great and we are happy.'

She was just counting her blessings. That is a precious lesson.

Although confined to bed, Vishnu Sharma would continue giving tuition to those looking for departmental promotions and for students appearing for the civil services. He kept himself active and that is a lesson to learn. We probably did not go to a top school, we studied in Telugu medium and had very low academic standards, yet we learnt rich lessons. And that stood us in good stead later in life when we went through times of crisis.

College Years

After finishing intermediate, Raj would move to Bhimavaram where he studied engineering, while I continued in the same college in Nuzvid as a BSc student with mathematics as my main subject. As luck would have it, the year I was supposed to do my master's at Nagarjuna University, it was declared a zero year. This meant I would lose a year. Since I didn't want to miss an academic year, I went off to Sagar in Madhya Pradesh for my MSc in mathematics. That gave me a different exposure to life.

I was in Sagar for two years. It was a place where no one spoke English. I had come from a rural Telugu-speaking place to the Hindi hinterland and it tested my resilience and ability to cope with the demands and requirements of the place. I had been removed from my comfort zone to a new place, which was a huge experience in itself. In fact, within a few months, I had picked up some broken Hindi, enough to carry on a conversation.

While I was completing my second-year MSc, my father told me to focus on studying for the civil services and asked me to shift to Delhi. That shift to Delhi was in a different league altogether. The struggle to survive in Delhi was another huge learning experience. I joined Delhi University for a master's in operations research but my focus was on preparing for the civil services exams.

In all, I would be away from Nuzvid for four-and-a-half years; including the two-and-a-half years I spent in Delhi. Eventually, I would return to Andhra as staying and studying in Delhi was expensive. Among other things I also wrote the test to get admission into a law university and ranked fifteenth in the Andhra Pradesh State Law Entrance Examination.

By then I had almost made up my mind not to sit for the civil service exams but had still enrolled in a coaching centre in Visakhapatnam. Prasanna, the friend I have mentioned before, had also enrolled in the same coaching institution. A few weeks into the course we realized what a sham it was. This centre promised the sky but when it came to delivery it was pathetic. There were no other teachers to talk about and all they did was dictate notes. We were disappointed. Then one day, while Prasanna and I were chatting, we wondered how it would be if we started a junior college, and how we would go about it differently.

In those days, residential junior colleges were in vogue in Vijayawada, Guntur and Nellore but the concept had not caught up in Visakhapatnam yet. I went back and discussed the idea with Raj. He had completed his engineering course and was involved in the family business but liked the idea. I suggested to Raj that we start a junior college. Prasanna too was supposed to join us, but he got selected in Group 2, Public Service Commission Examinations. Raj and I went ahead and started Vikas Junior Residential College in Visakhapatnam in 1993.

So, that was how it began, a journey where enterprise and education would be partners in equity. Of course, a lot of legwork and research would precede the actual founding of the institution and it would be a difficult ride, not least because of finances, but the two of us, young and ambitious, were determined. Backing out was not an option.

As they say, once you decide, the universe conspires to make it happen.

The Journey Begins

Neither of us had any money nor any experience of running a college. We did some math and found that we needed a minimum of Rs 4 lakh to start with. Through family connections we sought advice from the founder of an institution, who told us to always remember three things. The first thing he told us was not to start a business in partnership. His reasoning was that when the business starts reaping profits, it would inevitably lead to conflict over who would take the credit; and if it failed, the issue would be about who would take the blame. He went on to say that if Raj and I wanted to remain friends, we should not get into a partnership.

The second thing he said was that in any enterprise related to education there would always be parents who would blame us if something went wrong. But if we tried to prove the parents wrong, we would lose the student. So, our job was not to prove the parents wrong; rather, we should learn to swallow our egos.

Third, he said, if there are two partners, one has to play the benevolent role while the other takes a more aggressive approach, just like in a family. And, invariably, it is the one who plays the benevolent role who gets the credit. Throughout our journey, we remembered these suggestions and have benefited from them.

Raj and I picked up valuable tips from elsewhere too. We went to other institutions, some successful, some that were not doing so well, just to understand what they were doing. The research took us six months before we started but that bit of homework helped. Our learning has been continuous even after that. But it was tough to begin with. We couldn't mobilize the Rs 4 lakh that we needed. We eventually managed to raise Rs 3.5 lakh and started Vikas.

Our next challenge was getting the numbers. Thankfully, we managed that. We had planned to have 200 students and we got 196. We also made it a rule that we wouldn't admit beyond that number and that we wouldn't take students who had scored below 60 per cent in their tenth-class exams.

We had to work very hard to get good teachers. We did our research and went to different people well known in Visakhapatnam, and during these discussions we picked up names. We made a list of subjects and possible teachers. With that list in hand, we approached some senior people and said we wanted these teachers. They would look at the names and ask us why these teachers would join our junior college. Our stock reply would be, 'Because we want to build an institution.'

By this time Raj's father-in-law had been posted at Visakhapatnam as the regional director of homeopathy and we tapped all his contacts. We also contacted all our relatives who had migrated from other districts. All this happened organically.

Vikas had got under way, our first foray into education as an enterprise, that too in a place different from where we had grown up. That's another takeaway from this period: at some point or the other, we need to move away from our comfort zone if we want to learn and grow.

Many years earlier, Shomie too had to move away from the comfort zone of home learning to a boarding school in Dehradun. What he picked up in the process would stay with him. Let's go back then and find out what he learnt at Doon School.

13

Dawning at Doon

The Second World War was over. The machine guns had fallen silent; so had the swooping roar of fighter planes and the sporadic bursts of ack-ack fire. Germany had surrendered. Japan had been bombed into submission under an unfurling mushroom cloud. Shomie was too young to understand the global impact of the atom bomb but recalls that the "sense of bigness" was inescapable. He was going on eleven and, if the world was changing, his own little world was about to change too.

Shomie had been schooled at home for most of the first ten years of his life; then a message had come from Doon School in Dehradun that they had a place for him. That would be the beginning of a new phase in his life, a journey he would retrace many years later in a different capacity – as a master. Back then, though, it was as a student excited at the prospect of a two-day train journey and the necessary concomitants of life in a boarding school.

"I still remember that a list of clothes was sent and I was taken to the tailors and measured up. We also went to Calcutta's New Market to buy all sorts of things, including a dressing gown that was part of the clothes list. That was the first time I was going to boarding school."

The excitement wouldn't last long. "My father took me to school by train, dropped me, said thank you very much, goodbye and have a good time. I was lost sitting on my bed, my hands and legs trembling, and wondering what I was going to do," Shomie would recall many years later.

It was different from anything Shomie had experienced before, packed off to a new place, far from home, with strangers to share his room with. He had two roommates. While he was from Bengal, one was from Uttar Pradesh and the third boy was from the Northwest Frontier. That meant three little boys, from different parts of the vast subcontinent, thrown into a room together to find their feet in completely unfamiliar surroundings, an early rite of passage towards self-sufficient fellowship that every hostel student goes through. And then there was the impending test.

Shomie remembers that day. Some memories never fade but this one was important for a different reason. Years later it would help shape his approach to how schools could put students at ease. At that time, however, he felt totally lost. "Very soon, word came that I had to appear for an exam and I didn't have any clue what the test would be on."

Shomie flunked the exam. But he needn't have worried so much. "I failed the test. There were two other boys from the Northwest Frontier. One of them got 'G', even lower. The school said they did not mind what our standards were and that they just wanted to know that we were the right age. And, accordingly, they would decide which class the student would go to. I was put in 'F' form. Very quickly I learnt the ropes and got promoted to 'E' form and then I didn't look back."

An Idyllic World

"How would you describe your time at Doon School," I asked him one day. Both of us were in a good mood as Oakridge was coming along nicely.

"It was wonderful," he replied. "We would be taken for walks, near the river, in the hills. It was amazing and I learnt a lot about the valley. It is a beautiful valley, situated between the Shivalik Hills and the Lesser Himalayas; to the east was the Ganga, and to the west of the valley was the Yamuna. These were the boundaries and we grew up there among the trees. I learnt carpentry, machine work, bookbinding, leather work and stone carving. I won a prize in painting. All the craft classes were open on Saturdays and Sundays. Unlike today, when we can go out to movies or buy food, those days there was nothing. So, we used to go to the craft class and learn. I made a little steam engine that worked. I remember I made a dog out of wood. Learning was enjoyable and, although there was no pressure, examiners did evaluate us. We had what is called the 'Honours Book'. At the end of each term we would be in the Honours Book, for good behaviour, for good studies and good exam results."

What if the boys stepped out of line? Shomie laughed as he recalled the times he had to bend forward a bit – for the convenience of the teacher's perfect 'putt'.

"There was this gentleman called Jack Gibson. He would do wonderful things but would hit you on the bottom if you did something he didn't approve of. He called them putts. What I learnt in school then would be considered antediluvian today. We have got to remember children are growing much faster. They do know their rights. But it is good to show the current crop of teachers how we were taught then. I still have the essays I wrote. They were marked by Mr R.L. Holtsworth who taught us English. Every fortnight we had to submit an essay and it would be meticulously marked with comments. That was how thorough the teaching was. We would even go to his residence and listen to Wagner. There were other boys doing well and I had to do well. So, there was that competition between kids, which was again quite healthy. Moreover, the homework we were given had to be done by self-study. There was no other person to help. So, we learnt to study on our own. We had a very good library too and we would go, sit there and read. The librarian would suggest books and, in the process, also got to know our interests. So, our learning was huge. That was apart from all the different things the school would lay out for you. I learnt to play the sitar and appreciate Western classical music; I learnt to draw and paint too and was taught by a famous artist called Sudhir Ranjan Khastgir, whose paintings are now national treasures."

The outdoors would beckon too. "We would go rock climbing, go on mountain treks or raft down rivers and even go hunting in the forest, basically shooting jungle fowl with tiny pellets. Our time was filled with activity and we were never bored."

For Shomie the student, life at Doon School was like an idyll where education was both learning and entertainment. It was, as he says, a "wonderful experience" that would leave a lasting impact on him. "Among the things I learnt in school, the most important one was teamwork. You had to work with other kids, not just while playing a game but even when you were climbing a mountain or rafting down a river. We had to work together. So, I learnt a lot about teamwork, about taking risks and how to minimize the downside inherent in every risk. We also learnt how to manage our budget. Money would be scarce, so we learnt how to use money judiciously. That taught us a lot. Another key thing I learnt was the important quality of leadership. When you wanted to do what you wanted to do, you had to lead. When you wanted to lead, you had to convince people and bind them together. I learnt a lot about leadership in school, so much so that I became the youngest house captain. And then my father took me out of the school."

That would be sometime in 1951. Six years had gone by and Shomie was now a boy of sixteen. How time had flown! He would have loved to continue at Doon but had to defer to his father's wishes and return home to Calcutta. Leaving Doon was painful but recompense would come in other forms – and in multiple ways – enough to fill an adolescent heart. Shomie remembers the time, as clearly as if it were yesterday.

Senior Cambridge, College and a Special Friend

It was December 1951 and Shomie was appearing for the Senior Cambridge while hoping to continue in Doon School at least for another year to get the higher school certificate because his father had said he would like to send him to Cambridge. His father had approached Cambridge and Shomie had to get a higher school certificate before they gave him admission. "Senior Cambridge class is akin to Class XI. So, a higher school certificate would mean one more year. That's why I was expecting to stay at Doon but I think my father felt I really ought to spend more time in Calcutta before leaving for Cambridge. But perhaps the more important reason was that school was getting to be expensive. I left school that year without saying goodbye to my friends. It was a bit of a blow to me but I think I had the potential to go up the ladder in Doon, being a house captain, school captain and things like that. Anyway, back in Calcutta, we were all together for Christmas; my sister and I, and her friends and my friends. Our exams were over and we had all passed. So, we went on a picnic to celebrate. It was at that picnic that I met my wife-to-be, Pheroza."

Shomie had suddenly become animated. "I was seventeen and Pheroza was eighteen. I fell in love with her, there and then. That was a fairly emotional time. You know, when you are young, you want to hang around, wanting to know, wanting to go further. Looking back, it was rather a lovely time." Shomie recalls that at this time, he started taking an interest in politics. He had relatives who were fairly closely connected with the Congress party, while an uncle of his who had been at Cambridge, Indrajit Gupta, was a member of the Communist Party of India. He says that while Gupta never actively spoke to him about communism, Shomie became interested in the ideology. He felt that "this was the done thing". While he never joined the Communist Party, he was an activist in their youth wing. Back to Shomie's post-Doon School days, he studied physics honours at St. Xavier's College before joining Cambridge. Shomie says, "But I don't think I learnt much at St. Xavier's because the quality of teaching was poor, although the college had some good lecturers too. At Xavier's it was a loose system, except that you had to mark yourself present in class. That was a funny thing. The lectures in physics were boring.

We would go through books on mathematics but were not shown anything. I was bored and that also set me thinking if I could do better than that. Later, when I became a teacher, I realized how much I could do to make physics interesting".

He talks about a particular incident at St. Xavier's that has stayed with him. "We had a Physics Club where I read a paper on electrostatics. I tried to make it interesting but the paper was a flop; the physics I had learnt in college was of little use. And the main reason for that was I had not been taught to think for myself. I had been taught how to learn physics from the blackboard.

"While I was at school, I used to think of becoming a teacher. That fondness for teaching came from the wonderful teachers we had at Doon. But when I went to college in Calcutta, I was disappointed. And this Physics Club incident convinced me that one could transmit knowledge in better ways. That sort of strengthened my resolve to become a teacher."

St. Xavier's, then, was not a happy interlude for Shomie. Fortunately for him, this period would soon be over. While still a student at St. Xavier's, Shomie got admission to Emmanuel College, Cambridge, and completely lost interest in college. He didn't do very well in BSc Honours, being far too involved with his circle of friends, apart from politics, which meant going on strikes and things like that. But he got his degree in two years and then left for Cambridge in 1955.

14

Magic of Mentors

Nineteen fifty-five was a turning point in Shomie's life. For Raj and me it was 1993. That was the year Vikas got under way, the first landmark in our journey of education with a difference. As with all such ventures, this too was difficult to begin with, and it may have ended as an abortive attempt had some people not stepped up at the right moments. But who were these people? I call them mentors. Our success is largely because of having the right mentors at the right time. We were fortunate too in the sense that while mentors can guide you in some direction, it might not always be in the direction of growth.

An early mentor we consulted was Chigurupati Varaprasad. That would be sometime in 1992. Chigurupati Varaprasad ran the Sri Krishnaveni Educational Institutions.

Being in the field of education, his advice was valuable to us. He was the one who had told us not to get into a partnership if Raj and I were to remain friends. That didn't stop him from lauding our endeavour when Vikas was an up-and-running institution.

Varaprasad was a Lions Club Global director and even at other forums he would present our story as a case study and say, 'I was wrong in my advice, but I feel totally happy about their success.'

Another early mentor was Ratnakara Rao, who happened to be an uncle of mine. He was a businessman and told us to be first sure of what we were doing, then follow our instincts and not get carried away by what others said. It was my uncle who gave us the initial seed money as a loan and he would later advise us in our venture.

Looking back, it's remarkable that we were never short of advisers. Take, for instance, our auditor, K.J.D. Srinivas, who has been with us for thirty years now. When we started Vikas, we were naive and did not know what partnership meant or what a company meant. Our auditor friend wrote our first partnership firm deed. Not that he would limit himself to matters financial; there were times when he would double up as counsellor too. Whenever we hit rock bottom, he would divert our attention and take the discussion on a tangent.

I'll give you an example. It was many years ago, a time when Vikas was hardly making any profits. Our total turnover then was Rs 20 crore and our expenditure was Rs 20 crore; we were not making a single penny. We were clueless about how to survive. At that time, the Chaitanya group of institutions was making a profit of about Rs 100 crore. We would be admiring the Chaitanya group when the auditor would pipe up and ask us, 'Sir, can we think of acquiring them?' It would make us laugh. In a way, he made us see what our potential was. There were times when he believed in our ability more than we did ourselves.

He gave us one piece of important advice that I have always kept in mind. And that is, place matters. I'll come back to this in greater detail later in this narrative. For now, let's just say K.J.D. Srinivas made us feel glad that we were in Visakhapatnam and not in Nuzvid.

In retrospect, we think he is the one who put in our mind the seed of Hyderabad as a possible location for a future enterprise. He also talked about Mumbai and New York as potential locations, but it was the suggestion of Hyderabad that stuck. We realized that the place you function from can make a big difference. I have always kept that in mind. Now, when I look back at Oakridge, I realize that none of this would have been possible in Visakhapatnam.

In hindsight, the move from Nuzvid to Visakhapatnam was the passport to greater things – a graph that would be reflected in our journey from Vikas to Oakridge. But then Oakridge may not have happened without another man, our greatest mentor, Shomie.

We met Shomie in the year 2000. Till then my entire knowledge about education came from my interactions with senior teachers who were working with us. When Raj and I met Shomie, I might have possibly asked him a thousand questions. He had answers to almost all of them. There were times when I would visit his house in Dehradun for three to four days and talk with him, morning and night. That is how we started Oakridge.

'Zero Worth' to 'Potential Value'

There would be other mentors, too; people who would come up with timely suggestions about the practical aspects of doing business. One of them was Devineni Suresh who enlightened us about our potential value. Suresh, who was also from Nuzvid, was associated with Meenakshi Constructions, one of the top property developers in the country.

Sometime in 2007 or so, when we were stabilizing a little, Suresh asked us what our growth plans were. We told him once we get a grip on the financials, we would start a school, maybe two or three years down the line. He told us to go for fundraising and private equity.

But I was clueless when Suresh asked me for some financial data. We did not know how to read a balance sheet and did not know anything about financials. Then he told us about what our potential value was and said we could raise equity and start straightaway and grow. In hospitals, he explained, we count financials based on the number of beds; similarly we could arrive at financials based on the number of students.

Till then we had thought ourselves to be of zero worth; now here was a person saying that we were worth some amount. Our whole world changed.

Since then Suresh has continued to advise us on many of the financial aspects of going about a business. But for his intervention at that time, we may not have expanded Oakridge the way we did.

Another person who played an important role in our journey was Rakesh Gupta. He was our vice-president (strategy). He was from IIT Kharagpur, had gone to the US and worked in Microsoft, come back and done his MBA from the Indian School of Business. At ISB campus interviews he got selected by McKinsey. He completed his ISB course but there was still some time left before he was due to join McKinsey. Two of his professors referred him and he worked for us to conduct a Parents' Satisfaction Survey.

That was in 2008 or 2009. That is how our relationship developed. We told him he could join us if he wanted to, but he took up the McKinsey offer. Within four months or so, he quit McKinsey and joined us. He felt that McKinsey was a big pond where he was just a small fish and would hardly learn anything. But if he worked for an entrepreneurial organization like ours, there would be scope for him to learn. As far as we were concerned, we were keen to professionalize the organization but didn't know how to do it. That is how Rakesh joined us and he would be a critical factor in our transformation.

Transformation is crucial to any entrepreneur's growth trajectory. It was the same with Raj and I, both from the point of view of our evolution as entrepreneurs and in relation to the organization we would establish, People Combine, primarily an education services company that at one point owned both Vikas College and the Oakridge brand.

Classmates Again

At the discussions we had, Rakesh would bring up financial modelling, Excel manipulations and so on. Raj and I had no knowledge of such things and we would find the discussions difficult to follow. Then ISB started PGPMAX, a management programme designed for senior executives and business owners. Rakesh suggested we join the course, which we did and completed in 2012. Joining the course, which included eighteen months of intensive education, was another turning point in our lives. Thanks to Rakesh, other people of equivalent calibre and similar vibes would join our company.

All those we subsequently hired would be interviewed by Rakesh. That is how we were able to transform People Combine from an owner-promoter-driven organization into a professional enterprise. Rakesh has since left our company and started his own business but remains associated as an independent director.

At a more perceptive level, we were no longer out of our depth in the complex world of commerce and enterprise. Because both Raj and I went together to ISB, we would weave our classmates' stories into our efforts. It was also a continuation of our intertwined stories that began with our childhood as classmates in the same school many years ago.

Before giving us admission, the interview board at ISB asked us who would run the business in case both of us joined the course. We told them we would be able to manage. We could convince them and got admission. Both partners doing the course together was a kind of case study by itself. It was good both of us did the course or our conversations would have become stilted. And it was only after we did the course that we took private equity.

One of the requirements for private equity players is to have an independent director on the board. And that was how another mentor, Harikiran Vadlamani, would come into the picture. Harikiran Vadlamani joined us as an independent director in 2013, recommended by Suresh Devineni.

Actually, we had asked Suresh to come on board as the independent director, but he said he was anyhow there to guide us. Harikiran – we fondly call him Guruji – was a successful entrepreneur. He was part of KSK Energy but exited that around 2008. Now he has started the Indic Academy, a platform for Indian culture that has been doing fantastic work, both in the country and across the world.

Many people in our long journey played a key role in our transformation. They came at the correct time and made us what we are today. Every relationship turned out to be such a blessing.

Today, many people who are in education or otherwise, come to me or Raj for advice. Raj spends half his time mentoring people. We both love to do that.

What a transformation it has been! There was a time when we sought out mentors to guide us and now, the same people seek us out as *their* mentors.

Coming back to People Combine, that too has been a transformation, from one stage to another. When we started the Vikas Group of Institutions, it was a partnership firm in which Raj, I and our spouses were shareholders. We converted the same partnership firm into a company. Oakridge School and Vikas College were both owned by the Vikas Company. Later, in 2010, we changed the name of the company to People Combine.

Now, we needed to differentiate between all our brands and the corporate entity. Vikas College was one brand and Oakridge another. Then we started playschools under OI (Open Interactive). We also entered the hospitality industry with 7 Midway Plaza, on the Vijayawada Highway. All these brands were owned by People Combine.

We exited from Oakridge and OI in 2019 and shut down Vikas during Covid. We already had two Westberry schools in Tenali and Bhimavaram. We started Coschool after our exit from Oakridge. So, today, we have the Westberry schools, Coschool, 7 Midway Plaza and some infrastructure and real estate businesses under People Combine. In all, we had five Oakridge schools; two in Hyderabad (in Gachibowli and Bachupalli) and one each in Bangalore, Visakhapatnam and

Mohali, Chandigarh. When we exited the Oakridge brand, all of these were international schools and the top ones in their respective cities.

Who would have thought that two small-town boys, brought up in modest circumstances, in semi-rural surroundings, would have accomplished so much? But none of this would have been possible without those who helped us.

So, here's a vital tip, lest anyone missed it: one needs to choose mentors wisely because they play an important role in any successful journey.

I'll pick up this thread later. For now, let's go back and catch up again with Shomie, this time in the hallowed precincts of Cambridge.

15

Cambridge Chronicles

If life at Doon was an idyll, Cambridge would be the cradle of Shomie's future calling. The few years that he would spend here would go a long way in shaping his ideas about education and teaching and more importantly the teacher's unstated role as career guide and counsellor.

Away from the university, and the necessary tutorials it offered, there would be other learnings too that Shomie would pick up over these three years, all valuable life experiences that would broaden his worldview and which may not have been possible in a less flexible academic system.

Shomie acknowledges that when he talks about his days at Cambridge, where he studied physics, physical chemistry and metallurgy as his main subjects. "I studied for a natural science degree and could have done it in two years but took three years instead. And because I took three years, I had an easier time studying. On the other hand, I had a good time learning."

In a few words, Shomie had effectively summed up the concept of learning that he would eventually put into practice later as teacher, headmaster and principal: that education was essentially a comprehensive process and not merely a race defined by the score sheet. Even better if that process helped bring low-on-esteem underdogs out of their kennels of self-doubt. But Cambridge also ensured that while students had enough freedom, academic or otherwise, by the time they graduated they had learnt what they had primarily come for.

"You know, NP, in Cambridge, the system was really extraordinary," he told me one afternoon as we chatted over a cup of coffee. "On the same subject you may have three professors who would give lectures. You would be asked by a tutor to attend a particular lecture. So you went to whichever lecture you wanted to. There was no system of marking attendance for these lectures. You went or you didn't go. So, sometimes, we would skip early-morning lectures. It didn't matter at all. What was rigorously followed was the system of allotting supervisors. We were allotted a supervisor in each subject and the supervisor would give us work to do. We had to spend one hour every week with the supervisor who sat with students one-to-one, or one-to-two, and went through the work the student or students had submitted. This was a unique system. Very few universities offer that kind of one-to-one learning."

Then there were the Nobel Prize winners Shomie got to interact with. "Can you imagine, a Nobel laureate willing to spend one hour with me!" Shomie would recall. I could feel his excitement. Nearly seventy years on, he still hadn't got over that sense of wonder.

Valuable Life Lessons

Shomie would get to pick up valuable life lessons too in the years he was at Cambridge, experiences that would help him transition from a young adult into a mature individual at home in the world. A lot of his time was spent not just on learning but also in socializing. One of the great qualities of universities like Cambridge is that they had an enormous number of events and games and you could take part in them. Shomie had the ability of getting along with people and very soon he was invited to join some clubs.

One of these clubs was the Pagans, which played village cricket. Shomie and the others would go around the surrounding villages and play cricket with local folks. They would play on the village greens where they had daffodils growing and cows grazing, a perfect picture of the English countryside. Sometimes, it would be the village blacksmith who would turn out for the local side. A lot of learning took place at these interactions and it gave him a very good understanding of Britain and how it worked.

He also got a chance to earn money and travel. "I worked during the Christmas holidays, once as a postman's assistant in Hoban in London. In those days there would be a huge amount of mail and so they hired students. We had to sort the letters, carry them, follow the postman and put the letters in cubbyholes. I earned quite a lot of money and in the evenings we would go to a pub in London."

It was fascinating to hear him talk. And it was amazing that he still remembered these experiences. "You have an incredible memory, Shomie," I told him during a pause in the conversation.

"It's the quality of the experience, NP," he replied. "Fortunately for me, it was positive experience." He paused, before coming up with a question. "Do you want to hear about the time I worked as a lumberjack?"

Now, this was a surprise. With his twinkling eyes and diminutive frame, Shomie isn't someone you would normally associate with the profession of a lumberjack. Shomie must have sensed what I was thinking.

"Aah, NP, you don't believe me. But I actually worked as a lumberjack in Sweden." He laughed. "There was a Sri Lankan by the name of Gamini Goonasena (who later went on to play for Sri Lanka and then became an ambassador) who asked me to go to Sweden with him. He said there was a job. The job was to cut trees but not with mechanized tools. I asked a Pakistani friend, Tariq Hussain, to accompany me. They paid us by the number of trees we cut. On the first day our hands bled and there were blisters and I think we just cut half a tree. So, we went to the owner of this teak forest company and told him we were students, not like the tough fellows used to cutting trees. The owner said he did not want us to cut trees but prune the saplings and trim the trees. We got paid £5 for a day's work, which was a big amount in those days. At the end of one month I had £1,500. Then we took a train and went to Vienna and other places and had good fun. That was one interesting trip I did as a student."

Car, Calais and 'Clink'

Shomie was having the time of his life. He was in his early twenties and enjoying the freedom life offered. But it wasn't always smooth. One day, Shomie was in a pub where he met two Irish boys from Trinity College in Dublin. They got talking and by the end of the evening had decided that they should not part company.

"But is it possible to make friends so easily?" I asked.

"Everything's possible when you are young," Shomie replied before narrating another of his many experiences.

"They asked what I was doing the next morning and I said I was going to Spain. They said they would like to join. I told them I would take my car, although I did not have one. So, the next day, I bought a car for £25 and ten days later we piled into this car and chugged along. We crossed the Channel and reached Calais. That was the time Britain and France had landed troops along the Suez Canal, which Egypt had nationalized. I had reached Calais with my passport but without a visa for France. The French authorities decided that I might be a spy and they put me in the clink. I had my friends with me and, after twenty-four hours, I rang up the Indian High Commission in the UK where Vijaya Lakshmi Pandit was our high commissioner. Her nephews were my friends in Cambridge. The French authorities let me go but said I had to get out of France in forty-eight hours. So, we drove in this ramshackle car all the way to Paris and got stuck. We stayed there for ten days. Then we decided we better go to Spain and I drove all the way to Bordeaux. This is about 800 kilometres from Calais. We were of course stopped there but were finally allowed to leave.

"These were some of the experiences I picked up in my student days, which taught me so much about life, about meeting people of other nationalities, about earning my own money, seeing beautiful cities like Vienna, Cologne, Paris and Barcelona. What fun we had. These are really my Cambridge experiences. I learnt a great deal as a student – about how to live with very little money and survive, and how to make friends. I learnt to be a lumberjack and a postman; these are invaluable experiences students should have."

The point Shomie was trying to make was that learning comes from exposure and everyday experiences; that unless one steps out into the big, wide world, their education would be incomplete. Cambridge afforded him that freedom but made sure he utilized it with responsibility. That would be one of his biggest takeaways from his university days.

For Shomie, Cambridge was one of the greatest learning experiences that he had.

"Did you face any racism?" I asked him once.

"Never," he said. "It was a liberal place and I even remember taking part in demonstrations against the government over the Suez crisis. Many of us thought the invasion was wrong, so we took out processions."

Generations at Cambridge

Cambridge had started attracting Indian students towards the closing decades of the nineteenth century. One of those who had crossed the seas was Shomie's great-uncle, a brother of his paternal grandfather. The next to set sail was Shomie's father. Shomie was the third from the wider family, followed by his daughter. And today, his daughter's son is also at the same university, making it five generations at Cambridge!

"We all went to the same college in Cambridge, for four successive generations. Another thing that I must mention is that my college, Emmanuel, really fostered a respect for history in me, even that of family. Can you believe that they gave me the same room that my father had lived in, which was the same as the one my grandfather had stayed in as well? The whole idea of Cambridge was that students were there to seek knowledge and to do research. Some of the world's most famous scientists grew out of that system, among them James Clerk Maxwell and Isaac Newton."

Shomie's eyes had an animated sparkle. It seemed he had gone back to his Cambridge days and its ambience of deep learning. It was the same pull that had many centuries ago attracted students to the university, where scholars from Oxford had migrated in the early years of the thirteenth century following a dispute with local townsfolk.

"I think we all wanted to go to Cambridge, so we applied to a college that we knew and they also admitted us. The education in Cambridge was open-ended in that you didn't have to go to lectures, you didn't have monthly exams. We had an exam at the end of the year; that was the only exam you ever wrote. In between you constantly wrote papers; got them corrected and had professors talk to you about ideas and things that were taking place. The result was I got interested in radio astronomy."

It was in this environment of learning and exploration that Shomie began his final year at Cambridge. "In the final year every student had a tutor. The tutor would ask the student what he or she wanted to do and then arrange meetings with the Appointments' Board, sort of like today's Placement Cells. I told my tutor I wanted to be a research scientist."

But the leap from student to research scientist would not happen in Shomie's case. Life had other plans for him.

"My tutor nodded his head and said it was not a bad idea," Shomie recalled. "But he also told me I would not shake the world of science. And that was a great comment, which went deep into my soul. To me it meant that while I would not shake the world of science, I was capable of shaking the world in something else. So, I lowered my sights. I had already thought of being a teacher and decided to go into school-teaching, but not to just any school."

A tutor's comment had changed the course of a young man's life. A day would come when this young man too would mould lives, but with greater sensitivity.

After Cambridge, Shomie's next destination would be Gordonstoun in Scotland, which would mark the beginning of his journey as an educator and mentor.

16

Cashing in on Confidence

If the situation weren't so serious, we would have burst out laughing. The man looked like he was going to have an apoplectic fit if we stayed a bit longer. So we took our leave before he booted us out.

It was the year 2000, or Y2K, as it was more fashionable to say back them. Raj and I were already in the field of education for six to seven years with Vikas but we had no idea how to raise funds for starting a good school, as we planned to.

We had tapped our friends and extended families but succeeded in raising only about Rs 2.5 crore. That was in no way sufficient but that was the only money we had. We were also worried because we were getting into the school venture without thinking of consequences. Taking a loan was the only other option. The total cost of the school project on paper was Rs 26 crore, over five times more than the Rs 5 crore then needed to start an engineering college, or the Rs 15 crore required to open a medical college. We were clueless;

where would the money come from? So we went to a bank for a loan.

Raj and I both knew the bank's general manager, but he was aghast when we told him why we had come to meet him.

"Are you crazy to start a school by investing so much?" he sounded incredulous. "Not only will I not recommend your loan, I recommend that you do not get into such a misadventure."

So, back to square one. But there was no going back for us. We had already spent the Rs 2.5 crore we had raised on buying land, which meant we now had to build the school, come what may.

As if lack of adequate finances wasn't enough, another problem cropped up. We had already paid for the land, when the master plan for Cyberabad was drawn up by the government. The plot was right in the path of a road and so we had to request the landlord to return the money and he took a very long time. In the meantime, we had to buy another plot.

By then the project had taken on a momentum of its own. We had given the advance for the new plot to start the construction of the building. But since we had already announced the opening of the school, we started it from a rented property near the Jubilee Hills Check Post in June 2001.

The first Oakridge School had got going but the troubles were far from over. By the time the plan for the school was approved, the master plan by the state government had been rolled out. In between, land prices had gone up. But since we had already started the school, we had no other choice but to continue with the project.

We even started regretting our decision to start the school without financial closure. Just when it seemed the project would flounder, help arrived. A consortium of four banks gave us a loan of Rs 10 crore about a year and a half after we had started the school. We had come very near to calling it quits. Had we listened to common sense and naysayers, we perhaps would not have started Oakridge. But then, at times, your own ignorance and madness turn out to be a blessing.

Investors' Instinct

Another blessing was our instinct for investment, crucial to any business. In our thirty years of entrepreneurship, there was never a day when there would be Rs 1 lakh in our bank balance. It was like day one when we had started without any money and taken small loans from friends and family to start Vikas. And whenever we made some money, we would put up one more campus, open a new centre, go to a new city, bought a site, or construct a building. We always reinvested the money we made. As a result, we never had any cash reserves. Rather, the reverse was happening and we had huge loans, which were growing every day.

What that meant was that till our exit from Oakridge, we were always in a cash-starved situation. People around us thought we had gone crazy. We would keep borrowing, not only from banks but also from friends, and paying interest on the loans. I would also take loans from my wife and pay back with interest.

It was not an easy journey but, luckily, our personal life was frugal. For long years, till nearly 2012, I lived in a rented house paying a rent of Rs 10,000. That was the sort of controlled living we had. We shared a car and kept our personal expenses low while putting every penny into the future growth of our business. For many years we could never pay the bank interest on time and used the three months' grace period, making the payments only on the 90th day, that too only a part of the payment. And we borrowed even to pay the interest.

Our unsecured loans were piling up but we were willing to take that risk. Our families and network were fairly large, our intentions were always right and people too knew that. As a result, if somebody needed their money to be returned, we would tell them that we would pay them back the next month. We would then go to somebody else and get the required money.

For a long time, till 2016 or 2017, my credit card would always be 100 per cent outstanding. I used to just clear whatever amount that was the minimum payable. We were that stretched. Till 2017, I had the highest limit on the credit card in those days, which was Rs 15 lakh or something like that. That card was fully used, but never for personal consumption, only for productive, meaningful purposes, to ensure wealth creation or for children's education.

A key factor that would over time lend solidity to our enterprise was investment in land. I had learnt from my father that investment meant investing in land, not in jewellery or liquid assets. When it was our turn, for many years, our investment was only in expanding the business. Like, if we had one campus, we would start one more, whether it was for the junior college or later for Oakridge. Those plots and buildings were the underlying assets of our business. Luckily, we were in a business where there was a need for land and buildings, which resulted in an appreciation of their value. And because we insisted on paying the full tax on our earnings, without opting for exemptions that many claim by creating not-for-profit societies, we have legitimate claims to our assets today.

In this case, both Raj and I held the same values. Pay your taxes and be happy! That is how we thought.

Shared Values

Our similar values would help us maintain our integrity in other ways too. This is a small but important example. It was 1997, barely four years since we started Vikas. We had also just announced new campuses in Rajahmundry and Tirupathi, so the results of the Intermediate exams were important for us to attract students to our college. Then, someone approached us with leaked question papers and offered us the "opportunity" to buy them. But, of course, we didn't. We felt it was unethical. We were in education, teaching morals and values to our children; buying question papers for the survival of the institution was not right.

The people who were selling these papers even told us we could pay them after the results. But we stuck to our decision. Most of our competitors bought the leaked papers and later landed behind bars. Fortunately, because our value systems were the same, neither one of us was tempted for a second.

It's true that we were struggling to stay afloat but our wider goal was to serve the community as a whole. I usually give the analogy of a curry-leaf plant. When a curry-leaf plant is very small, you water it, nurture it with fertilisers and it slowly starts growing. Curry leaf is an ingredient one uses every day, especially in kitchens in southern India. If you pluck two to three leaves every day, that plant will never grow. Its growth thus gets stunted. Once you plant it, you must keep nourishing it. Your kitchen requirements can be met by purchasing the leaves from outside. In a few months, when this plant turns into a bush, you can pluck as many leaves as you require; the plant's growth will not get stunted. Even if the whole community starts plucking its leaves, it will still continue to grow and serve everybody's purpose. So, if you can hold yourself back from the initial temptation of plucking those early leaves, it will serve your needs and the whole community's needs too. Delayed gratification or, rather, the ability to delay gratification is an important life skill and tool for success and wealth creation.

It is similar when it comes to financial and wealth management. We followed that discipline. As a result, when we exited from Oakridge, we not only got fair returns, the people who gave us loans or were our shareholders over the last twenty to twenty-five years or were associated with us, also got their share of gain, which, for them, was unbelievable. They never expected such returns.

'Sheer Providence'

But all this would not have been possible without Shomie. I have said this earlier too, and saying it again. Meeting Shomie was sheer providence.

When we were in Visakhapatnam and running Vikas, our students were bookish, learning by rote and only keen on scoring marks. Raj and I were both unhappy and would talk about the quality of students that our feedstock schools, the education system, seemed to be churning out. From those discussions came up the idea of how it would be if we started a school and how different it could be. We wanted to explore what made a good school. So, Raj and I started visiting schools.

We visited all successful schools, starting from Coimbatore to Dehradun, and also big schools that were miserable failures. We would try to analyse why they had failed. If we found a school that was perceived as successful, we would try and understand what made them successful in terms of nurturing students.

Many times we would just walk in saying we were seeking admission for our children. Schools are funny; if you walk in as a parent or guardian, they welcome you with a red carpet. They will give you all the details that you need. But if you want a formal appointment, as someone interested in opening a school, it takes years. They think you are trying to take a share of their IP.

As I have written earlier, we got to know about Shomie when we had visited Doon School. After our Doon visit, the three of us returned to Visakhapatnam, where Shomie would eventually meet us for the second time. We took him around Vikas and showed him what we were doing. Shomie, in principle, agreed to associate himself with our project.

While this was going on we were simultaneously working on a concept note, which showed that the project would be capital intensive. The second issue was if we invested so much in the school, would Visakhapatnam be able to provide the returns. The choice was to either reduce the specifications or start the school in Hyderabad. We decided on Hyderabad. We had started Vikas in Hyderabad the year before.

Shomie referred us to Vijay Gupta, an architect from Delhi, and came up with suggestions about the kind of curriculum we could have. That is how he has set up so many schools, around fifty to sixty after his retirement, not only in India but also in places like Indonesia.

So, that is how our dream took shape; touch-and-go for almost the entire period but always backed by self-belief, and the necessary interventions at the right moments. That is destiny: inscrutable, apparently indifferent and a seemingly unrelated tangle of loose ends.

One such loose strand was already in place in faraway Scotland. Neither Raj nor I was in the picture yet but Shomie was. Very much so.

17

The Scottish Incubator

Shomie was interested in a man called Dr Kurt Hahn, who had started a school in Germany called Schule Schloss Salem. When the Nazis came to power, Hahn wrote a letter to all his old boys, one of whom was Prince Philip, the father of Britain's future king, Charles III.

"If you have anything to do with the Nazis," Hahn wrote, "you have to resign from the old boys' association."

A letter like that is unlikely to escape the notice of the authorities. This too didn't and soon the Gestapo, the dreaded secret police of Nazi Germany, began tracking Hahn, all the more since he was a Jew.

But Hahn had powerful backers. One of them was Ramsay MacDonald, then the prime minister of England, who arranged to get Hahn out of Germany. Hahn then settled in Scotland where he founded Gordonstoun School in 1934.

Hahn had interesting ideas about teaching, which went well beyond classroom learning. Every institution, he would say, needs to have just two pillars on which they should stand. One was a sense of honour and the other, a sense of obligation to that institution. He also thought it was important to have a curriculum that, apart from the common subjects, should teach children to rescue people in distress, such as when they are trapped in forest fires, mountain disasters and shipwrecks. So he set up a fire service in the school, run entirely by the boys with the master in charge. A mountain rescue service ran in the same way like the coast guard service, which was already there because the school was on the sea. According to Hahn, taking part in a rescue in peace time was morally equivalent to fighting for the country during war.

It was natural that a person like Shomie, with ideas brimming in his head, would seek out Hahn. "Hahn was getting to be known and I was interested in his ideas about teaching," Shomie would recall during our conversations regarding Oakridge, which was then still in the conceptual stage. "So I applied to Gordonstoun and met him through the Appointments Board. There was a teaching position and I was interviewed by the headmaster who had just taken over from Hahn. He appointed me. So off I went to northern Scotland to teach in Gordonstoun."

"So Hahn had already retired when you joined Gordonstoun?"

"Yes, but he still lived there. He was keen to meet all young teachers to talk and discuss his ideas. He would sit with us and indoctrinate us in a sense. I used to play tennis with him and have debates."

Shomie taught physics at Gordonstoun. He eventually rose to become head of the physics department and started building his radio telescope. He applied to the Royal Society and got a grant. The condition was he had to involve senior boys in his project, so that they got a feel of what scientific research was.

For Shomie, fresh from the intellectually stimulating ambience of Cambridge, Gordonstoun would be a different kind of experience, a return to the fundamentals, so to speak.

"What was it like?" I asked him one day.

"That would take a whole afternoon." He laughed.

"Take the entire evening," I replied.

"All right, NP," he said, "you asked for it."

Then he began. "Gordonstoun was a spartan school, with no luxury whatever, not even heating. It was very cold but we survived. And, among the things that we had to do, which was Hahn's idea, was that all students must go for a run at six in the morning to loosen their limbs and get blood circulating in just a pair of shorts, nothing else. And then they would come back and have a cold shower. After the cold shower, they could have a warm shower. So, that was what we had to do, including the young masters. We had to run with the kids."

"Did King Charles III have to run too?"

I tried to keep my expression as deadpan as possible but the question was waiting to be asked. Very few teachers have the privilege of teaching a future monarch. Shomie was equal to the question.

"Well, NP..." His eyes twinkled, "Charles was not a king yet."

The Gordonstoun Way

Coming back to Gordonstoun, the system there got Shomie hooked, especially its stress on certain values and principles that every student had to aspire to.

"It interested me a lot," he continued. "A boy who joined the school didn't get the school uniform until he was judged to be worthy of it. And to be worthy, you had to know the school song and you had to show that you knew what your obligations were. At the end of the term, all the new boys who had joined at the beginning of the term would join a big ceremony and they would be given the school uniform. Then they felt they belonged. Secondly, there was no corporal punishment. The punishments were all, again, based on obligations. So, if you did not do your homework or were guilty of some other lapse, the house teacher concerned would ask you to tell your housemaster that you hadn't done your homework. And he left it at that. The boy was obliged to; it was his honour-bound duty to go to the housemaster and say, 'Listen, I haven't done my homework and I have been sent by so and so.' Then the housemaster would take appropriate action.

"The punishment was 'walking'. Depending upon the severity of your crime, you were sent on a walk and the walk could be for 3 km up to 10 km, as deemed fit for the crime. But you had to walk only when you were free, not at any time. So, you did your walk without supervision. No one would ask if you had completed your punishment walk. But you had a little diary in which you ticked off that you had gone for the punishment walk. The diary was confidential. No one could see it except yourself and the housemaster.

"Among the other obligations were, 'Have you brushed your teeth', 'Have you done your 100 skips', 'Have you made your bed', and other such stuff. The student was taught to be a responsible person. I don't think such a system would work now. Even in Gordonstoun it did not work 100 per cent. But it worked to a large degree. Even those who cheated would sometimes not cheat. It got into your system.

"As you grew within the hierarchy and got more and more responsibility, depending upon how you discharged your responsibilities, you got a stripe. After the school uniform that you were given, the next important thing was the stripe. One of them was called a white stripe. You not only had obligations but the responsibility to see that other people were doing things the Gordonstoun way. And these were all elective posts. And then you got a purple stripe when you were elected a colour bearer. That means you were found fit by the community of teachers and boys for wearing the colours of the school. You couldn't even play for the first XI of the school until you got your stripes. Yes, students would strive to get their stripes."

Shomie paused. The words had come in a torrent. It was evident how much of Gordonstoun he had internalized. A part of that experience would go into the making of Oakridge, though there would be three other schools in between.

Fighting against Yourself

"Another thing I liked about Hahn," Shomie continued, "was that he was sure that one of the obligations of a school like Gordonstoun was that it had to cater to the local children. It gave its fields to the local children to play games. And it went out of its way to organize these village children into doing things for which they got a badge, which was called the Murray Badge. I don't know whether you have heard of the Duke of Edinburgh Award. This award was given by Prince Philip to those boys who had achieved certain standards and you could have a bronze standard, silver standard and a gold standard. Murray Badge was a forerunner of the Duke of Edinburgh Award.

"The Duke of Edinburg Award is run in India as the Indian Youth Award. You have certain standards to achieve to get that award. For instance, you have to do a one-night trek on your own with your own mates and camp and make your own food. Then you had to do community service. You have to judge your own physical abilities. At the end of the day, you had a book in which you ticked off the standards you had to achieve. Actually, you were fighting against yourself constantly.

"I don't know if this system would work across schools in India, but my school did it. In India the schools are too hung up with marks. But what the Duke of Edinburgh Award teaches is leadership, it teaches risk-taking, being collaborative. So, it was another thing in Gordonstoun that I enjoyed very much. We had a strong emphasis on community service and rescue service. I would be taking a class and the fire siren would go off, then three boys from my class would leave the class and go. They would change in three minutes and they were away to fight, usually a forest fire. That was enormous."

Shomie would teach at Gordonstoun for twelve years. During this time he also worked with an organization called Nafi in Oxford to develop a subject called Physical Science at A level. The idea behind it was to combine physics and chemistry, freeing up an A-level student for subjects like English literature or history. That was another innovation the school introduced as part of a pilot project approved by the education authorities.

In 1961, three years after joining Gordonstoun, Shomie got married to Pheroza. After the wedding, held in India, the couple went back to Scotland where they started a family.

"Did marriage change anything for the carefree, idealistic teacher?"

"Nothing much." Shomie had laughed. "Except that we were very poor. I used to get a salary of £35 a month, hardly enough for a family of five. From that I used to give my wife £4 a week for food and other expenses. Out of the £4, she paid £1 to a lady who would come to help her. But she was happy there. She had even learnt to drive and once a week she would go to the market in Elgin, which was 8 km away."

Learning beyond the Classroom

Coming back to Gordonstoun, Shomie would pick up other valuable ideas too, especially ways to make learning interesting. "Kids need to get out of the classroom. The concept of shutting them for five hours a day within four walls was quite unnatural. You have to allow them to go for games or physical activities. It was compulsory for children to get a 40-minute break after two classes, before they went back to a new class. That was another thing that I felt was important to do with children. Even today, I criticize schools for the number of hours they keep children locked in classrooms. I think it is shocking. So, Gordonstoun for me was very much an incubator of ideas in education. There, I learnt the value of teaching children through adventure, teaching children through hands-on projects. So, there I built my radio telescope."

Shomie would also take his students outdoors, climbing peaks that were 4,000-foot high, right by the sea. "We would climb two or three of these peaks in winter during the weekend and challenge ourselves. Those excursions taught me the value of adventure training and how it brings out the best in kids."

If you remember, I have written about his interesting experience when he had taken fourteen boys to climb a peak called Ben Alder. Shomie and his boys had camped at the bottom of the peak for the night and set out the next morning. To remind you, a severe blizzard had started, with a strong wind. The blizzard had frozen their eyelids shut, which meant they were climbing without seeing where they were going. And on their right was a sheer slope.

Shomie recalls that they only had a map and a compass. And that an otherwise unprepossessing student led the whole group to safety. He speaks of this incident as illustrating once again what he knew instinctively – that children rise to challenges.

"Kurt Hahn used to say this with a twinkle in his eyes, 'You have to put children where they feel some risk to their lives. Only then can they strengthen their real character, when they have to look after their lives.' Of course, it doesn't mean that you put them in danger. But where they felt that if they weren't careful, they could get hurt, they are careful. That was a great learning."

Shomie would leave Gordonstoun in 1968. It was not something that he had planned; rather, it was a phone call that would send him back to India. The call was from his former teacher in Doon School, Jack Gibson, who was then heading Mayo College, a private boys-only boarding school and one of the most reputable educational institutions in India.

Gibson was on a visit to England when he dialled Shomie. "I am retiring and want you to take over from me," he said.

"Sir, what a lovely thought," Shomie had replied. "But don't think I will go all the way to India for an interview."

"I didn't ask you for an interview," Gibson had shot back. "Just come."

So, at the age of thirty-three, Shomie packed his bags again for another long journey, this time to Ajmer. Gibson had sent him a colour photograph of the main building in white marble, with a top tower, and, in his own words, Shomie "fell for that".

Pheroza was sad. She had become used to life in Scotland. But Shomie had made up his mind. "I had decided to leave also because of a man called Enoch Powell who was talking about rivers of blood because of immigration." Powell was a Conservative British politician known for his controversial anti-immigrant rhetoric.

"Large numbers of Indians had turned up and were taking jobs," Shomie said. "He wasn't accepting the fact that no one was willing to do those jobs other than immigrants."

Whether it was politics or the call from a former teacher, one of the twin roads to Oakridge had taken a decisive turn towards eventual convergence. Mayo would be the first stop in Shomie's journey back to Dehradun where Raj and I would meet him, though that was still thirty years in the future. But what was future for Shomie was present for Raj and me. So back to the future again.

18

Turmoil to Triumph

Shomie's journey has largely been an exploration and a widening of horizons. He is a thinker whose mind has been like a laboratory, churning up ideas on how to make learning interesting.

Ideas would also drive Raj and me, but in a manner that was often reckless. For us, the journey has been one of struggle, of short-lived ups and long periods of down, but always propelled by the desire to do something different. Looking back, it's a miracle that we succeeded.

How did we succeed? If you ask me, it's primarily because of two or three reasons. One is, we were at the right time at the right place and in the right field. While there was a lot of hard work, the element of luck also worked for us. That we had the right mentors was invaluable to our journey. I see this aspect also as a miracle. The third aspect is that although we were always short of money, we had enough people and institutions to support us. They genuinely believed in our commitment.

But belief in our commitment alone may not have sufficed had people also not had faith in our sense of integrity. Part of the reason was that even as we borrowed money from friends and family, we would repay whenever possible. We would also return the money immediately if someone we had borrowed from needed it urgently. But there were also people who kept their money with us for almost fifteen years.

Not that it was always so positive. Just when we would be in the middle of a crisis, some of our lenders would start getting worried. That was the time when some people would begin asking for their money to be returned.

But we kept going, pushing our luck and pressing forward. So, while such things were happening, we built the Oakridge campus in Visakhapatnam. This was 2008. Mind you, this was a time banks were reluctant to lend to us. But, as I said earlier, there were people who believed in us. Our builder not only constructed the structure, he also completed the entire campus without us actually paying a penny to him. It was only after we got the bank loan that we would reimburse him.

We faced another crisis while building the Oakridge, Gachibowli campus in 2001. That was also a nightmarish time. Banks were not willing to lend, whereas we had committed to pay rents while we were building our campus. It was a financial mess. But many vendors and agencies actually waited for almost a year to get their money back from us. In the meantime, we continued to borrow at a high interest rate, which was a huge risk.

We could have gone bankrupt around this time in 2004, when we approached the executive director of Andhra Bank for a loan to repay our outstanding unsecured loans. While visiting Visakhapatnam, the executive director had a talk with M. Venkatrao, a shareholder, who told him, "If you are to lend money to them, it is as safe as keeping it in the bank itself."

It was then that Andhra Bank gave us Rs 6.5 crore just to repay our unsecured loans. That would be a huge turn in our entrepreneurial life. That gentleman may or may not remember that he told such a thing to the executive director but, for banks, even a small whiff of our struggles could have wiped us out.

Around this time, one of our partners decided to leave. He wanted our assets to be valued and his share paid off to him. That put us under even more pressure and we had a traumatic time. But we crossed that bridge too.

Like a Story

When we were planning to build the Bachupally campus in 2009, we did not have money even to buy the land, forget about constructing the building. So, we met the landlord, told him we had no money to buy the land and asked if he could still register the plot in our name and that we would pay him whenever we had the money. It reads like a story.

The landlord accepted our proposal after we paid a token amount. But a lot of it was overdue. We had not learnt anything from past experiences and were again into loans. What happened was that the unsecured loans kept increasing year after year. The previous year's unsecured loans were Rs 10 crore. The following year the amount had risen to Rs 15 crore. The result was we again became financially weak in the process of building the two campuses at Visakhapatnam and Bachupally. But every experience brings with it new learnings. In this case, it was the realization that borrowing from individuals had its limitations and that, along with institutional funding, we needed to go for equity. We would do that when we started the project for the Oakridge, Bangalore campus in 2012. That's when we took private equity from a proper financial fund.

Actually, we were learning throughout our journey. Both of us were first-time entrepreneurs doing business intuitively. Had there been formal structures in place, we would not have probably been able to do some of the things we intuitively did. In our case, growth happened by learning as well as through intuition.

Our ISB stint worked too as we learnt the business jargon and language. In the process, we also started going to a new set of consultants and advisers. So, in between Vikas and Oakridge, we had transformed ourselves into professionals. By then, we were conforming to legal compliances and other governance standards. We had matured quite a lot.

But progress or expansion, struggle and borrowings were our constant companions. Till 2004–05, Raj and I hardly drew any salary. This was because, as we grew, our unsecured loans grew too. While we were getting funded on the one hand, we were still borrowing to service the loans when our internal cash flows were not sufficient. That ensured there was nothing for us to take home as we were also reinvesting every rupee that we would earn.

We started drawing salaries around 2005. But till 2011–12, our salaries were hardly Rs 3–4 lakh a year. It was only after 2011–12 that Raj and I started drawing salaries that were commensurate with our effort. Till then, many of our employees drew much higher salaries than we did. After all, they were being paid the market rate; otherwise, it would not have been possible to hire them.

In 2019, when the Oakridge transaction happened, people saw us and were wowed. But this is not something of a miracle. It was twenty-seven years of continuous hard work. During this journey, anything could have gone wrong any time.

While we were expanding, we were also internally doing our mental maths. We had an idea of the possible value of our physical assets as well as our outstanding loans. In the worst case, we would have been left with little money or even nothing. Had everything gone wrong, we would have paid off everyone, closed shop and restarted our life. But throughout this touch-and-go journey, we always made it a point to pay our employees on the designated salary day, which was the fifth of every month. It was something that we scrupulously maintained.

Element of Trust

That brings us again to the third factor in our eventual success: trust. Not defaulting on salaries and repaying individuals whenever we could were a part of the mutual trust that people had in us and which, in turn, would prompt them to lend a helping hand without the slightest hesitation. There were times when vendors of our hostel mess would continue their supplies for six to seven months without us paying a penny. If I have to make a list, there are hundreds of people who have helped us because they believed in us. I think that so many people believing in us is a miracle. I also see it as a measure of our sincerity which people understood. They had trust in us and we conducted ourselves as trustworthy people.

Let me give an example of how our stakeholders trusted us. There was a time when we had to ask many senior teachers of

Vikas to leave because of our financial crisis. They joined other organizations but continued to be shareholders in Oakridge. It was only after Oakridge changed hands and the transaction took place that they got the value for their shares – in some cases more than fifteen years after they were asked to leave.

Letting these senior teachers go was difficult but we really had no option. There had been a bloodbath where big players had paid huge amounts to students who had done well in their Class X Board exams. The system was to "recruit" those students – that's how coaching centres produce rank holders year on year! That year had been particularly "memorable". Anyway, in such a market, we really could not afford the senior teachers. It was a calculated decision that required courage because word goes out and next year's admissions could become difficult. But then that could happen only if we survived the current year.

We were also watching and learning and did not want to commit mistakes. We had let go many teachers at Vikas in 2002, the year the bloodbath happened. It's true we were growing at a fast pace but realized that our competitors were financially strong and had huge businesses. So, we consciously decided to slow down on that front. We wanted to remain sustainable and profitable than get into any kind of competition. Another decision we took was to change from the state board to the CBSE board as we were looking to capture the niche market from eastern India. The bloodbath was happening only in the Andhra market, not elsewhere, and we were still getting students from outside. As a result, we did not go down in terms of finance; we went down only in volume and market visibility.

In the meantime, two things happened with us. One, we started Oakridge, although no one had any clue as to what Oakridge was. We were building its foundation and fundamentals and growing on the Oakridge front, albeit slowly.

On the Vikas front we had already shifted to the CBSE board. This was a different market altogether. That way people simply forgot us. It was only after Oakridge started making news that people noticed and thought that we had done a smart job. People thought we were like the bear, hibernating for some time and then making a reappearance. What we were actually doing was different things on different fronts and constantly repositioning ourselves.

19

The Education Lab

Shomie joined Mayo College as principal in 1968, following the call from his former teacher Jack Gibson. It was the beginning of a new chapter in his life, one that would set the ball rolling towards our eventual convergence, although that would be another three decades away. But the stage had been set. If Gibson had not made that phone call, Shomie may have remained at Gordonstoun. Had that happened, there would have been no Oakridge.

This is what I had meant by a parallel, back-and-forth narrative when I began this biographical account, because this is essentially one story – of Shomie's development as an educator and his conception of Oakridge and of how Raj and I facilitated that.

Coming back to Shomie's six-year stint at Mayo, it would be the first laboratory where he would test out the ideas he had picked up at Gordonstoun.

"Here was a new chapter in my life. I was young, all of thirty-three, brimming with ideas, and here was a school, which though a very good school, was antediluvian in many ways," Shomie recalled one day as we talked about his days at Mayo.

It was a freewheeling afternoon of reminiscences, one of the many we have had since we met at Dehradun on a providential visit to the city in the Himalayan foothills. "It must have been a great honour, Shomie, to get the call from Mr Gibson," I said, bringing up the topic.

"A great honour and privilege, NP," he replied. "I sent my family home and then went straight to Mayo College. I joined them after completing my term at Gordonstoun as head of physics."

"What was your first impression of Mayo?"

Shomie smiled as he gathered his thoughts. "The school had old-fashioned ideas, somewhat like *Tom Brown's School Days* kind, but I was impressed with the staff and the boys. Which meant I had the material with me to start changing things. It took me a little while to understand the mechanics of the school but when I did, the first thing I did was to give the senior boys more freedom to take decisions on their own."

Shomie had started with adventure training as he tried to bring in more outdoor activities. He also wanted the students to get into more project work. And since he was keen on electronics himself, he set up an electronics lab and started new methods of teaching science.

In the six years he was at Mayo College, from 1968 to 1974, Shomie made a few interesting changes in academics. Basically, while the structure remained the same, he tried to change the attitude of the teachers and make learning more interesting, liberal and more enquiring.

"Most of the students were children of defence staff, railway employees, etc., with their parents in transferable jobs. A large number were children of Rajput princes and that was one group," Shomie recalled, dipping yet again into his vast reservoir of memory.

"Recently, I went to the fiftieth year of my first batch, the 1969 batch. It was interesting to see that there were lieutenant generals and senior army officers. The principal was a former lieutenant general, who was my student. And there were bureaucrats, and people from various levels. I was delighted to actually see this group. They were my first lot."

The Sanawar Years

Shomie left Mayo in 1974 after a serious disagreement with the board of governors regarding staff salaries and staff terms and conditions. He felt that the school was charging a pittance from the students, which was creating problems when it came to upgrading the institute. Shomie was without a job for some time when he got a call one day. The person at the other end was the education secretary in the central government. The bureaucrat told Shomie that the headmaster's post in a boarding school in Sanawar, Himachal Pradesh, was vacant and asked him if he would be interested in the job.

The vacancy was at The Lawrence School, one of the oldest and most prestigious boarding schools in Asia. Although an autonomous society, it was still governed by the Union education ministry and the chairperson would always be the incumbent secretary for education.

"I was excited but I had one condition: I would not go for an interview," Shomie said. "They agreed, saying I had to come and meet the board of governors. So, I went to the education ministry and met the board. It so happened, half of them knew my father and it became a bit of a conversation that had nothing to do with the school. They offered me the job and I went off with my family in an open Jeep, all the way to Sanawar. I never regretted going there."

"How hard was it to leave Mayo?"

"I was not upset that I left Mayo College," Shomie replied, "but I felt, maybe, I had been a bit too impetuous."

The school in Sanawar was designed for children of those who worked for the army and the navy. It had started as the Lawrence Royal Military Asylum for children of senior officers who could not educate their wards in England. An indication of how famous it was comes in Rudyard Kipling's novel, *Kim*, where one of the characters tells the eponymous young protagonist, the Irish orphan Kim, "We'll make a man of you at Sanawar."

Shomie has fond memories of the school, and not only because of the picturesque view it offered from its 6,000-foot-high perch on a hilltop. "Those were the most wonderful years, though the school had its own systems because of its military background. I realized that I needed to continue with some of these old traditions and not upset the apple cart. This is something I learnt after my experience at Mayo College. They had a ceremony called 'Trooping the Colour', basically a parade in recognition of the fact that it was a military school. In the olden days the students would naturally join the military; though fewer students do that now."

The first change Shomie brought to the school was to make it less regimented, considering that the students were constantly marching. The second thing he did was to make it a proper co-education school. "Boys and girls would attend the same class but that is where it ended. There was no socializing between them, except in the classroom. They would even eat their lunch at separate tables. Then I decided to build a larger dining hall so that the girls and the boys could eat together. I felt eating together had a socializing effect. I got the first donation of Rs 1 lakh from Raunaq Singh, a parent, and built a beautiful dining hall. It is now called Raunaq Hall. That was one of the first steps I took to make this school more liberal. Then I started reducing the regimentation, but gradually. There was a lot of resistance, not so much from the old boys, but from the staff. Senior staff found it sacrilegious."

Developing Leadership

Another key change Shomie would bring in at Sanawar was, what he called, the pattern of thinking. "I realized that the teachers were not seekers of knowledge; they did what they were told. I had to change the pattern of thinking. I also brought lots of changes in how the students could develop leadership. One of the things I did was to send them on camps for six days, where they would go with a teacher on a preplanned route. It could be trekking, climbing, etc. For Sanawar this was probably the first experience of this kind. Earlier, they would have camps where students would live in a tent without any sense of adventure or bonding and no one would show any sense of leadership. Remember what Kurt Hahn had said? 'Always put children at risk to their own lives.' This is how you develop leadership. I also introduced a lot more responsibility. I gave every child in Class XII a responsibility so that they could learn what to do in a community, as a senior. So someone was put in charge of the school hospital. She or he would go every day to the hospital to check on those admitted and check if they were being fed. Similarly, I put students in charge of the dining room and the library. Every year I would rotate the responsibilities so that everyone had a hand in everything. It was a novel idea which I tried out."

Shomie enjoyed the complete freedom he had in running the school. "You know, I even started a mushroom farm and a chicken farm for the boys. I started showing them how they could produce biogas. We used the biogas for cooking, for street-lighting and all sorts of things. Then I got into serious trouble when the government found out that I was selling the mushrooms and the eggs and not paying sales tax. Oh gosh! That was serious trouble."

Only those incorrigibly serious would have missed the glint in Shomie's eyes.

He had another run-in with the authorities, which was truly serious and could have landed him in real trouble.

"The school," Shomie explained, "was a military school owned by the ministry of defence. When the defence ministry handed over the school to the education ministry, sometime in 1946–47, it had transferred all the guns and weapons to it. These were real weapons and we would carry them while marching up and down, like young soldiers, as part of NCC training. Then, in 1975, Indira Gandhi imposed the Emergency. That was a time when police would conduct searches and check everyone for arms. It was on one such search that they found this cache of 180 weapons! The school did not even have a licence to hold the weapons, though they were there when the school started.

"They wanted to arrest me. I told them I had nothing to do with the weapons. But the situation was serious. Even newspapers carried stories saying that weapons had been found in the school. Fortunately, the Union home secretary's daughter was a student of our school. When I rang up the bureaucrat, he complained that I had got him in a fix. We eventually got out of the mess but, for a while, I was truly scared."

Shomie would remain in Sanawar for fourteen years. Then, one day, L.M. Thapar, the chairman of Doon School, called Shomie and asked him to come over to Rishikesh. Shomie met Thapar at the chairman's holiday home. As they chatted, Thapar suddenly sprang the offer. "I would like you to take over the headship at Doon," he told Shomie. It was an offer Shomie could not refuse.

20

Map of Success

Shomie headed for Dehradun. It was the final bend in his road to Oakridge. But more importantly, it was the place where Raj and I would eventually get to meet him. In a way, therefore, Dehradun was an involuntary protagonist in the Oakridge story. But that's how it has always been. Place, or geographical location, does play a key part in our lives and is often the difference between success and failure. This chapter is about that aspect of our story: how choice of place played a defining role in our entrepreneurial journey.

It was K.J.D. Srinivas, our auditor and mentor, who pointed that out one day several years after we had started Vikas Junior College in Visakhapatnam in 1993. We were talking about things in general, looking back at the road we had covered, when he suddenly said that we would never have reached the position we were in had we started Vikas in Nuzvid, the place we belonged to. KJD, if you remember, was the person who wrote our first partnership deed.

"If you had started it in Hyderabad, that too would have been different," he told us. "The thing is when you are sitting in the state capital, the thinking will be very different. Similarly, if you were in Mumbai, instead of Hyderabad, your exposure would have been different. In Hyderabad people think Rs 10 crore is big money. In Mumbai, Rs 1,000 crore is considered big money. And, if you were in New York ... that again would have been different."

It was an interesting thought. Actually, KJD had put his finger on something vital to any enterprise – physical location and the associated socioeconomic milieu. While most of us think that success or failure depends upon our innate ability and hard work, there are many imponderables that are not in our control. Take, for example, a person in a strife-torn country where survival itself is uncertain, forget development. This person may have a fine business brain but his opportunities may be limited because the existential issues are different. So, if one has the luxury of choice, they should be in a place where there is scope for both thinking and doing big. The point I am trying to convey is that we cannot choose the place of our birth, but we can certainly choose where we want to live and work. And it's important we choose wisely because that can make all the difference between stagnant survival and robust existence and expansion.

KJD's words had stuck in our minds. So, a few years later, when we were thinking of establishing Oakridge, we decided that it had to be in Hyderabad rather than in Visakhapatnam. Hyderabad offered us the prospect of not only higher growth but greater visibility.

Earlier, when we were starting out, we had chosen Visakhapatnam as the place to establish Vikas because Vijayawada, had by then become fairly crowded and was a highly competitive market. That is why we started Vikas in Visakhapatnam, a city that was big enough but where the competition was not as stiff as in Vijayawada. We thus established ourselves in Visakhapatnam and made our ground strong for our future battles. Within Visakhapatnam we started Vikas in the city centre and not on the outskirts, where the competition would be less. In the centre, though competition is more, you are also seen as a major player.

The same principle would guide us when we came to Hyderabad, hoping to set up Oakridge right next to CHIREC School, the top K-12 (kindergarten to Grade XII) institution in Hyderabad then. We did not get the right plot but were still not willing to move away from the region and ended up starting Oakridge where we did. The price of the land was prohibitively expensive. There were pressures to relocate elsewhere as well as the temptation of land at a much cheaper rate if we shifted our planned campus a little distance away but we said nothing doing and opened the school right there. Things may have been vastly different had we not stuck to our decision to build Oakridge at the plot we had identified.

The same principle would again determine our choice when we set up another Oakridge, this time in Bengaluru. This campus would be right next to The International School Bangalore, or TISB, one of the premier schools in the city. Choice of location, therefore, has been a key component of our success. And that brings us back to the topic inextricably linked to the journey of life. And that is, success and failure, the twin plot points that anchor our future.

'Thank God I Was a Backbencher'

Failures, as the saying goes, are the stepping stones on the road to success. I don't know about others but, in my case, my early failures were instrumental in pushing me towards taking up education as an enterprise.

But first, here's a short list of my failures which, in hindsight, proved to be important. One, I was did not crack the Civil Services; two, I was unsuccessful in getting a visa to the US as a student; and three, I was a perpetual backbencher. But I thank God that I was a backbencher.

Let me explain. In those days, friends who were successful and meritorious students in the tenth standard got admission into polytechnics. The highest position most of those who went to these polytechnics would rise to was that of a supervisor in a workshop or factory. Those who were toppers at the intermediate level took the path of the staff selection board and similar examinations. Those who were successful at the undergraduate level went on to become supervisors at telephone exchanges or railway departments. Most of my classmates and friends, who were frontbenchers, got into those slots, leaving nothing for a backbencher like me. And because all those gates were closed, I had to keep walking to find my own path and, in the process, ended up being a co-creator of this story of education.

It's not that whatever we did was a success. After we started Vikas there were many small things we tried to do as part of the school but they did not work and we had to keep changing our approach. But that's part and parcel of any entrepreneurial journey. The key is to admit one's failures to oneself because the person who does that is the one who can adapt better and do things differently.

Fortunately for us, we got it right where it mattered most, by landing up at the right place – Dehradun.

21

The Last Lap

Looking back, that was the only way this story could have been taken ahead further. Shomie's journey from Sanawar to Dehradun to take charge as headmaster of Doon School was not only one of pride; it would also lead to his fullest development as an educator with a vision. His stint at Doon would toughen him up as a person too, one who could be uncompromisingly tenacious when needed. The beneficiary, needless to say, would be Oakridge.

"Of course, I couldn't refuse the offer to run Doon School. I was a boy there. It was a moment of pride to not only run my old school but also run a school that had been envisioned by my grandfather, Satish Ranjan Das. Yes, of course, I accepted," he would recall during one of the many conversations we had.

In Shomie's words, Doon School was a remarkable institution that was in many ways far ahead of its time. Many of its systems had been copied elsewhere, especially the idea of community service. "We were doing this in the year 1935 when nothing like this was there. It was part of the curriculum. Another was adult education where we used to teach the class IV staff how to read and write. And, when I went there in 1946 as a student, we had the Adult Education Society and used to do village development. We used to cycle on Sundays to a village called Tunwala and built some schools and things like this. No school had done this before.

"That was one aspect. Secondly, though the British system was still there, a huge amount of Indianness was there too. Our music was all Indian music. We didn't play any classical Western music. We all played the sitar, the dilruba, sarod and the tabla. We had some very good music teachers from Santiniketan. Sudhir Khastgir was our art teacher. The school was very much Indian in spite of the fact that there were gentlemen like Jack Gibson, John Martin, R.L. Holdsworth, all of them amazing teachers."

Shomie was fifty-two when he joined Doon School, with years of experience behind him and still a lot of time left to leave his own imprint before his retirement eight years later. "Basically, I continued in the way the school was being run. Of course, many of those ideas of Doon School had been incorporated in Mayo because the principal (Jack Gibson) was from Doon School, and also in Sanawar because I was there."

Shomie would get to introduce some of his own ideas too. One such idea was a separate building for Class XII students. He had noticed that the students were not prepared enough for the wide world when it was time to leave school. The reason was they didn't get enough exposure or enough time to take decisions on their own, a problem he felt was common to insulated schools of this kind.

"I introduced a separate building for the twelfth class, which was separate from the school. Here the boys from this class studied separately and lived separately and they were given freedom. They could decide on their own the kind of programme they wanted by consulting their tutor. The board of governors eventually thought this was too much, and the system was scrapped."

Tough Administrator

All the while, though, Shomie was evolving as an administrator who could be tough when needed.

"Did you face any political interference as headmaster?" I asked him one day.

"Nothing that I couldn't handle," Shomie replied. He recalled an incident when a movement was on to stop teaching of English altogether in north India. "This movement had picked on Doon School, which was an example of an English School. One day a man descended on the school with about 200 people and started shouting slogans. I asked him what he was doing and he said, 'You have to stop, this business of English.' I told him, 'All right. You have to talk to my boys and convince them. Why don't you come in, have lunch and then talk to the boys? Bring a few guests with you.' Five of them came and they sat on the tables. Every child spoke to them in Hindi. The message had gone home."

After lunch, Shomie got all the senior boys together and got the man to talk to them. He spoke for some time and then asked the students if they had any questions. Among those present was a former Doon School student who had graduated from Oxford and had come back to India to appear for the civil service exams.

"This young man," Shomie recalled, "got up and spoke, in flawless Hindi, 'I am like you from the Arya Samaj. My parents sent me here at great cost. Because I came here I could attend one of the most prestigious universities of the world like Oxford. The reason I could was my English was very good. You want to take this opportunity from us?' "The fellow went away. The next morning, I got a call from the chief minister. 'Das sahab,' he said, 'I want an admission to be made.' I told him, 'You are the CM. I can't deny you. But, from your side, only yesterday, you were saying that this school should be closed. Now, you want an admission to be made. I am not able to understand the contradiction.' The CM responded, 'No, no, Das sahab, don't worry, all these things keep happening.' The entire conversation was in Hindi."

Another time Shomie had come under a lot of political pressure was after he had rusticated the grandson of the country's president at the end of Class X. The boy had misbehaved badly. "I went and met the president in Delhi and said, 'Sir, this has happened and I don't want him back in the school because he is going to be a bad influence. And I think he is misusing his position as your grandson. I will see to it that he gets into another school but I am not going to keep him in this school.'

"The President tried to explain but I told him, 'You and I were both in Cambridge. You know what value systems are, and what value systems should be. And this is one of them. You should respect my decision. I am doing it not only for my school, but also for your grandson.'

"He accepted it. He said, 'All right. Thank you very much.'

"Two days later, the then governor of Uttar Pradesh called me. 'Das sahab, this student is the grandson of the president. Please don't expel him.' The boy's mother had approached the governor.

"'You have to reverse this decision,' the governor told me.

"I said, 'Sorry, sir. The decision has been taken. It has been approved not only by the board but by the president himself.'

"'I am the governor of UP, you have to listen to me,' the governor told me.

"I said, 'I am sorry. I respect you as the governor of UP, but I can't respect your command of doing the wrong thing. You can do what you like, but I am not going to reverse my order. The governor banged the phone down."

These were all tough decisions but leadership had lent steel to Shomie's character. Another incident that could have spiralled beyond his control happened during the statehood agitation for Uttarakhand. The agitators had shut all the schools in Dehradun and wanted Doon School to close too. Shomie had refused.

"How can I close my school? Where will the boys go? I can't send them home like that. It takes time to organize that," he told the agitators. When they insisted, Shomie invited them to his office for a discussion. "Three of them came. I told them not to close the school and said I would help them out. I told them I would take the entire school on a march in your support and will try and convince the other schools to do the same. But I put a condition saying they would have to stand in front of my boys and explain what this movement was all about.

"After that they timidly spoke to the assembly of boys and also the teachers and then left. They boys, on their part were keen to participate. On the day of the march, I called the TV and newspaper guys. When they came, I had the boys line up and explained my plan.

"The youngest kids, up to Class VIII, will walk out this gate, make sure they get photographed by the TV cameras and come in through the next gate. Those from Classes IX and X will go further and then turn around. The Class XI and Class XII boys will walk all the way to the Clock Tower – about a kilometre and a half – and then come back. But this would be a silent walk; no slogans."

The chairman of the Doon School board called Shomie when he heard of the plan. But Shomie convinced the board, saying that since the school was in Dehradun, it made practical sense to support the statehood movement. The next day it was all over the news that Doon School had gone on strike in support of Uttarakhand.

"I could see that a new state was being formed and we would be living in it. So people would remember that we supported them. That was one reason," Shomie would say. "The second reason was that I couldn't close the school. The other schools also participated but with teachers, not with students."

Return to Roots

In a way Shomie's move to Dehradun as headmaster was a return to his roots. His grandfather, Satish Ranjan Das, a barrister by profession, was the brain behind the founding of Doon School. It's an interesting slice of history that offers a glimpse into how a visionary mind works. This is what the grandson has to say.

"My grandfather wanted to start a school based on the British public school system because he felt that students of these schools were so trained they could serve anywhere in the world. While that served the cause of the empire, he anticipated that once the British left India, these students, imbued with the idea of service, could fill the vacuum in the administrative services."

Satish Ranjan had started a school, at Hastings in Calcutta, but that had failed. He then decided that he would go for a bigger project, a public school with boarding facilities where students from all over India could come. That's how it began. He collected over a million rupees and formed the Indian Public Schools' Society (IPSS), with the objective of founding public schools open to all, but died of lung cancer in 1928.

"It isn't recognized often that it was my grandmother, Bonalata Das, who pressed the Government of India to take the project forward. The government then took it up. Three persons played a key role in the founding of the school. They were Sir Joseph Bhore, IPSS chairman, Sir Akbar Hydari, the secretary, and an Englishman, Sir Frank Noyce, who was in charge of education. A plot was eventually found in Dehradun. It was the old Forest Research Institute situated over a 1,000-acre area. Frank Noyce and others later went to England, where they selected Arthur Edward Foot, a science teacher at Eton, as Doon School's first headmaster."

And, the Name's Oakridge

Shomie retired from Doon School in 1996. Four years later, someone from the school would call him up one afternoon to say that three gentlemen wanted to meet him. The three gentlemen were Rajasekhar, Dhanunjay and yours truly, Naga.

While writing this book, I asked Shomie what his first impression was after talking to us. Shomie had smiled before replying. "You know, NP," he said, "I was intrigued because you didn't come across as the kind who would have the funds to start a school. Even then, the cost of setting up a Greenfield school was close to Rs 30 crore."

After some discussion about schools and the likely cost of building one, Shomie had said the school he wanted to build would have an International Baccalaureate (IB) curriculum. We didn't know what IB was, so Shomie had explained that it was an enquiry-base learning system, with the curriculum designed by the International Baccalaureate Organization in Geneva. "If you want to set up a good school, I will help you get the IB," he said.

Later, after the project got under way, Raj and I had asked Shomie to suggest a name for the school. "Many years ago," Shomie told us, "I had applied for a research job in physics at Oakridge National Laboratories in America. Let's call this Oakridge."

Both Raj and I liked the name.

That brings us to the end of the book's biography section. Of course, many incidents, many memories have had to be left out because of space. What's there is just a basic account of our aspirations and struggles, and of how two roads, that originated nearly thirty years apart, converged to create a school whose reputation is secure even after the exit of its creators. But that is precisely how we had envisioned the school would be.

While the school took shape, Raj and I evolved too, from entrepreneurs to what can be called edupreneurs. In that sense, it has been a journey of transformation for us, guided by Shomie, our greatest mentor. And what a transformation it has been!

The book now moves to its next and final section, which is about our ideas about the path education might take in the years ahead.

SECTION III

BACK TO THE FUTURE

22

A Prologue

Over the last two sections and twenty-odd chapters, I have taken you on a journey of sorts. Rather, four journeys towards one end. That of Raj's journey and mine, individually and together, and then our path with Shomie, master and mentor. The course of these twenty-five years that I have walked you through has also largely mirrored the journey of education in India – from legacy schools to government and proliferating private institutions that serve all strata of society.

It has been a journey that should interest a social scientist. A changing world, India's demographics, the needs of a young and growing population and evolving regulatory frameworks have combined to make the education sector different in several ways from what it was twenty-five years ago. At the same time, delays in introducing changes and clunkiness in execution have conspired to keep several other things at almost the same point where they were a quarter of a century ago.

The starting point of the story of Oakridge was at this intersection of the old and the new, with the objective of forging a unique way forward. What then was the way forward? While Shomie, Raj and I agreed on several aspects, we all had our own perspectives on what lay ahead for education in India and, by extension, for India's future.

So far, I have been the raconteur for all the previous stories and thoughts shared with you. In this section, you will hear from Shomie and Raj about what the future holds in their own voices. Shomie, first.

23

Deschool the Roadmap

Shomie Das

It seems you want to hear from me what I believe lies ahead, or should lie ahead, for education in India. This, then, is both a wish list and a road map, if you don't mind the expression.

A society that is "deschooled" is my idea of the ideal.

What do I mean by "deschooled"? The Oxford Dictionary meaning of "schooled" is not "educated" or "taught", mind you, but "trained in a particular activity or in a particular way". Or, in other words, trained to conform. When the beauty of being human lies in our unique individuality, what can "schooling" achieve for either the individual or society at large?

This might sound strange, coming from a teacher of so many decades. But it is precisely because I have seen the education system from up close that I say this.

Coming back to deschooling, I cannot take the credit for coining this intriguing word. It comes from *Deschooling Society*, a wonderful book by Austrian author Ivan Illich that I highly recommend. In his 1971 book, Illich articulates his polemical ideas about modern education and talks about schools as places that, through their consumerism and system of institutional hierarchies, almost negate their original purpose – that of an individual's fullest development.

American author and educator John Holt, a committed advocate of unschooling, took Illich's ideas about education further. He said, "A deschooled society would be a society in which everyone shall have the widest and freest possible choice to learn whatever he wants to learn, whether in school or in some altogether different way." However, as tempting as this siren song of "widest and freest possible choice" in education is, in a country such as India, one cannot stray from formalized, institutionalized systems.

We must, of course, remember that Illich and Holt lived and worked in the context of the developed world, where education's primary function was not that of the most potent survival tool available. So, what do we do then in India to make the idea of deschooling appeal to both our instinct and logic? Perhaps, define deschooling as excising or, at the very least, minimizing the "particular" ways that negatively impact individual blossoming.

This means making the current education system as convivial as possible for the child, and working towards a greater partnership between parents and teachers.

Engaging with Parents

In the two earlier sections of this book, Naga, or NP as I call him, has taken you through how as educators we have individually, mutually and collectively tried to ensure the child's place at the centre of the institutions we have been part of; how we have navigated within regulatory frameworks and also advocated with the government on issues pertaining to education. NP has left the question of parents for me. And with good reason.

A more engaged partnership with parents is integral to my vision for the future of education. We must not forget that parents are the second-most important stakeholders in an individual's education. Often, their child's future, and even their own, is dependent on the said child's academic performance. This, as we know, unfortunately leads to parents exerting pressure on children, thus increasing the already heavy burden that children struggle under.

When parents become part of the formal education process, they begin to understand the different pressures on children. At Oakridge, we tried to involve the parents in a lot of activities – in the library for book recommendations, in the dining hall for recipes, and for career counselling as well. If one starts to think about it, there are endless possibilities and ways of involving parents as more than just anxious financiers of their children's education.

A better partnership with parents, where their participation ensures that teachers become facilitators rather than those who have to "school" the child, is the ideal scenario for a child to not just survive but thrive.

The Humanities Quotient

The one-sided science-oriented learning system in India is one thing I wish could be done away with. Take a Class XI or Class XII science student – they hardly go into any class where they are taught anything. It is only in the laboratories that they learn.

It is extremely important that students get a sound idea of subjects like history, geography and English. A sense of history and geography is integral to human knowledge and ability. I cannot stress enough the importance of understanding the geography of a place, the issues the people of the place face. It is important to read authors who have written about the place. All of this is vital to get a sense of the world we live in. It makes me sad to see children going to a place with no idea of the place. At the very least, they should know the connectivity, the history, the issues and the concerns of the place.

At Doon, we made it a point to teach children the geography of Dehradun. The mountains, the valley, how the rivers flow. We had a teacher, Gujral Singh. In those days, class tests would be written on the board and then the teacher would suddenly ask, "Name the bird that's sitting on the window." He would suddenly play Wagner and ask them to identify the composer. Can you imagine what this brought to a child?

Parents are our most important resources towards this end of nurturing a child to be more. I always insisted on meeting the parents. If possible, even visiting them, so that we had an idea of their home life. Do they have books at their home, is there music and laughter in their house? I understand that given the numbers in India, it is impossible for teachers to know all the parents, but we can and should try to get a sense of a child's background so that we can identify where the child needs our support.

Multiplicity and Diversity

What about policy? Over the years, governments have come up with reports and plans that are sensible and forward looking. For instance, the National Education Policy or NEP 2020 is well formulated and well meaning. As was the 1966 Kothari Commission Report. Sadly, the government does not have the power – even if it has the willingness – to push through recommendations.

One of the complicating factors is that education is a state subject and compliance with guidelines depends upon the state government concerned. Thus, uniformity of policy or implementation is missing.

However, in some ways, this has proved beneficial for India. For instance, the existence of different state education boards encourages multiplicity and diversity. This is reflected in the fact that a large number of students from boards across the country hold their own and do well in diverse fields, contributing significantly to nation-building efforts.

Several of our state boards have very good books – Telangana is one. The West Bengal Board is also good, as is the Bihar Board. The problem is in the learning systems that focus on knowledge-based education, not an enquiry-based approach, and thus rote learning becomes the "logical" tool to do well academically.

The Universe of Universities

Another mindset or practice that makes me unhappy is the tendency to shove people into the university system. This often slows down an individual. After Class XII, an individual should ideally have the skills to get and keep a job.

Universities, under the guise of providing choice, can straitjacket a person's intellectual development. And even in universities, we remain focused on what other people thought and said, not what we are thinking. How then will academic thought progress?

Let us take the US, for example. Their learning system is not knowledge-based and curiosity is rewarded. For instance, they allow accelerated learning for certain subjects – a child may be in Class V but do mathematics and physics at Class VII level. The system both enables and encourages that.

I have also seen schools where they divide their classes vertically. Standards X, IX and VIII are all in one physical classroom and the older children teach the younger ones, thus consolidating learning for those doing the teaching. Schools should be free to innovate, taking into account children's varying abilities and needs – in other words, to "deschool". And this is what I wish for in India.

Coming back to the mindset of university education as mandatory, in India we talk of "vocational education" with a sneer – they are for the poor, whether in ability or resources. However, in Europe and North America, choosing to take up a trade after school is not at all frowned upon. In fact, a certain measure of "earning your keep" is encouraged from early adolescence. With this comes a sense of responsibility, independence and, of course, confidence that cannot be measured in academic parameters.

However, at the end of the day, the numbers in India make most things an impossibility. The only system possible is to shove all the children within the confines of a classroom.

Four Walls and a Classroom

If there was only one thing I could change, I would change this: the system of confining children to within the four walls of a classroom. At Doon School, classrooms were allotted to specific teachers and these teachers remained in these rooms – the students moved around. This meant that after every 45-minute period, children could stretch their legs. Children need movement – it is important for learning and retention as well as mental health. Plus, this adds a bit of variety too.

Endnotes

Given the unique constraints we face in India, the diversity across socioeconomic and cultural strata, our sheer numbers, the ingrained mindsets and, above all, the absolute need to survive, the child is left with nowhere to turn.

With well-wishers all around them – parents, teachers, schools, the system and the government at large – we still end up failing our children. The rise of anxiety, depression and other mental health issues in minors, the rise in cases of suicides and the corresponding helpless frustration of parents all point to the pressure on children.

The answer goes back to the teachers, the classroom and the school. If schools could at least understand the benefits of a "deschooling approach" and work to limit the "particular" ways that negate the possibility of individuals blossoming, we could do so much.

For me, this means consolidating our beliefs in a school system where children are at the centre, teachers are facilitators, parents are partners and the government is an effective enabler.

24

Quotient of Love

Rajasekhar Yarlagadda

Naga has taken you ably through our stories already and Shomie has written about his hopes for a child studying in a school in India in the future.

What then is left for me to talk about? But I'll give it a shot. The road map for education in India is too vast and complex a topic for me to take on, so I'll dwell upon the simple things. Such as working collaboratively with teachers, parents and the government as edupreneurs to ensure that children learn to navigate through their lives with joy, love, compassion and dignity.

Seems like a tall ask? Not really.

I cannot and will not talk about systemic mindsets and practices but what individual edupreneurs, schools and teachers can work towards.

Mindset Mantra

The first is our own mindsets. We need to realize that employers look for social skills – these are the foundations of leadership skills. Leadership is not about technical skills – how much you know mathematics, physics, chemistry, or languages. Leadership is about the power to influence people. So, understanding people and communicating with people have to be worked towards.

The International Baccalaureate system rightfully stresses these and, thus, the children grow up to be confident, sociable and empathetic. But schools don't need IB affiliation to adopt this approach. They just need to think out of the box, that's all.

The Importance of Diversity

Another aspect where schools fail terribly in India is in acknowledging, addressing and including differences. This is all the more unfortunate because we as a country are so diverse.

One way of inculcating this sense of diversity is to ensure that, in a school, teachers represent as many states as possible. India has 28 states and 8 Union Territories, each with its distinctive cultural practices, festivals, culinary habits and languages. Schools must draw upon this cultural plurality.

At Oakridge, since financial considerations put a cap on the number of expat teachers we could hire, we engaged around ten interns from Europe for music, dance, foreign language training and so on for a stipend. They were not made class teachers right away. And this is how we started adding more diversity and giving our students a wider exposure.

Matter of Pay

This has already been spoken of but poor teacher salaries are a huge contributor to the gaps and lags in the Indian school system. If you compare the salary of a teacher with that of an IT professional, it amounts to almost nothing. Also, students from the southern parts of India are more geared towards pursuing medical or engineering degrees. Inevitably, this creates paucity of good teachers.

Most governments invest in professional degree colleges. So, once all the academically competent candidates enter engineering and medicine, the last set heads towards non-professional college degrees. And it is they who eventually become teachers.

But this is in the south, primarily. In the rest of India, especially in the east, large numbers of students pursue degrees in literature and the social sciences. We need to tap into this non-medical, non-engineering pool of candidates and ensure that they are paid salaries commensurate with other industries.

Teaching the Teacher

Teacher training is another absolute imperative. It's obvious that kids never learn from teachers they don't like or love. If a student has a favourite teacher, they tend to focus more on the subject that teacher teaches. It is not because the child loves that subject more; it is because of the child's liking for the teacher concerned. This interesting link – a child's liking for a teacher and the propensity to concentrate on the subject taught by that teacher – has been the focus of research studies.

At Oakridge, we regularly brainstormed on fostering a healthy relationship and bonding between teachers and students. We introduced several out-of-the-box or, you can even say jack-in-the-box, sort of initiatives. We made it a rule that every fortnight, teachers would have to play with the kids; not just cricket but simple old-fashioned games. There was a little resistance initially. Some teachers said, "Okay, every fortnight, the kids can go play and come back." I clarified that this would not do. The teachers have to play with the kids. That, though, wasn't the end of the matter. A few days later, the principal told me that if we did this every fortnight, it would be very difficult to finish the syllabus on time.

My response was simple. In a class of around twenty-five students, four or five would always be undisciplined. If we did this, we might discipline those students and also finish the syllabus. I managed to convince the principal and the teachers, and we began with simple games. Let me tell you that the exuberance of the students was something I, or they, will never forget.

Another unconventional initiative I took was asking the teachers one day to bring cooked food for their students. Maybe, samosa, poha, or whatever they liked. Some teachers said that they were not good cooks; some said it was difficult to get all the ingredients they needed to cook. I asked them to choose whatever dish they wanted to cook, and said the office would provide the necessary ingredients. I told them to just get a dabba from their home, put the food in the container and take it to class so that the students think that their teachers had brought it from home. This way, a child will feel loved. It didn't cost much to cook for twenty-five students, but the bonding that grew between the teachers and the students was something to remember and cherish.

Circling back to our philosophy, as children don't learn from teachers they don't like or love, schools can always work towards enhancing student–teacher bonding.

Partnering with Parents

Another aspect that schools must work on is partnering with parents. For instance, at a school where we had 3,000 students, I said that the teachers should invite all the mothers for a coffee meet at Starbucks. And we did call the 3,000 parents to Starbucks. At first, we envisaged this as a sort of parent–teacher meeting. But we realized that when ten parents meet up, they can often start finding faults with different things. We didn't want this. So, we identified some teachers whose people skills we trusted.

We also designed an invitation like this, "Dear…, I am happy to have your child in my class. But I want to know more about how your child is at home, how they behave and respond to different things, how much they play every day, how they divide time between TV and homework. This will help me understand them better and interact with them more effectively in the classroom."

So, the mothers started coming and talking about their children. But we didn't want to do that within the school environment. So, onwards to Starbucks. Every class teacher was to take their parents to Starbucks in batches. This too was great fun. The parents felt that the teacher cared about their children and were concerned about their development. That, in turn, fostered a bond where the teacher and the parent became a team, working together for the development of the child.

We must remember that such initiatives will at first invariably face resistance from teachers. No one likes change. But once the process starts, the teachers themselves will devise more such initiatives.

As Naga has already mentioned, I am a great believer in the love quotient. So is he, and Shomie too, though the phrase is mine. If we bring this quotient of love and joy to schools, children's confidence and compassion will blossom. Achievements, success and contribution will follow – for the individual, the family, the community and the nation as a whole. What more can we want?

25

Lessons for Life

Naga Prasad Tummala

As I have said repeatedly, my theoretical knowledge about education was extremely limited. And yes, here's a candid admission, my understanding and evaluation were all geared towards success in examinations; in other words, result-oriented.

Mind you, I am result-oriented even today. Otherwise, we wouldn't have survived in this hugely competitive domain, let alone thrived. But let me define what I understand by the word "result".

We built Oakridge as per Shomie's wishes and instructions and facilitated, as far as we could, his dreams in terms of creating for children an ideal place for learning. In the process I realized that, growing up, we had also lived the Oakridge model.

Sounds strange, doesn't it? Let me explain.

I am not talking of smart classrooms or even inspirational teachers, but the practical and spiritual underpinnings of a way of life that shaped our response to situations. At the Zilla

Parishad school where we studied, good teachers were a rarity. But constant interaction with nature and nonstop navigation through risks and challenges made our days so intense that we never understood the meaning of the word "bored"! We went to school, we went to the farm, we had domestic chores. And I talk of an entire set of people, not just Raj and I.

This gave us a constant sense of accomplishment. It was not systemized; it was all by default. Yet, while not much in the classroom made sense for me, we learnt many life lessons. If we didn't have this conditioning, this experience, this book would not have happened! A successful future is, thus, not necessarily the effect of academic learning only.

The 'AI' of Academics

Today, academic learning does not even require teachers. Teaching can happen through AI. This would be faster and better, with stronger academic delivery almost guaranteed. The important thing to note is that responsibility and discernment is not taught simply through passive, academic learning or even active academic learning. Humans are inspired by other humans – this is the primary role of teachers.

A teacher of the future is one who inspires learning. This can happen only if there is love of learning and a corresponding desire to involve children in that quest. That calls for a different level of dedication to nurturing young minds.

Educating for Change

Undeniably, most of the jobs we know today will be replaced by technology. It is equally possible that new jobs will emerge.

Only three years ago tech companies were hiring aggressively and offering sky-high salaries. Today, campus placements have gone down considerably, and even close friends or family cannot help one get a secure job. The very concept of absolutely secure jobs is gone. So long jobs were based on what you "know", but, tomorrow, it will be about how well you adapt. Thus, education needs to foster the ability to handle change and uncertainty.

We, in our socioeconomic stratum of privilege, provide our children perhaps too much security and protection. Thus, they grow up with a false sense of reality. After so many years of living padded within cotton wool, they are not prepared to handle the changeability of real life.

For me, the education of the future needs to enable children to handle uncertainty and navigate the shocks of change, to prepare children to live independently and to become productive, whether as part of a cohort of fellow professionals, a community, a country or as a citizen of the world.

Life skills and the ability to be independent are directly proportional to the success of an individual. Look at children growing up in underprivileged communities – they are adaptable, flexible, street smart and, yes, they thrive too. Children at all ages need to face appropriate risks and challenges. If we only protect them from suffering instead of conditioning them to handle suffering, they will fall at the first barrier. And then, we will have failed them. By "we", I mean the inextricably linked education system and parenting system. We need to groom for autonomy. And for this we need to reorient ourselves so that schools are not expected to be merely rank-generating factories.

The Reorient Express

Parents are not unwilling to change their mindset. When we started Oakridge and the parents learnt that there were no textbooks, they were shocked. But they adapted and became willing partners in the process. To summarize, true education in a changing world must inculcate the capacity for change. The present is unrecognizable from the past, and no one knows what the future will bring.

Also, we cannot blame the government for every drawback in the system. Governments in such a vast and diverse country as ours are doing what they can. Now, educators and parents must step up and foster a sense of learning and the ability to deal with change, while instilling human values.

Education will serve its purpose better if it is local, relevant, sustainable and leads to contentment rather than being global, irrelevant, unsustainable and which does not lead to satisfaction. The indices of success need to shift from material ones such as number of cars, bungalows and portfolios to a happiness index such as in Finland. Only then can we claim to have been educators in the real sense.

Endnotes

I have come to the end of my narrative. But before I finally wrap up, a few words on what made me write this book.

Multiple reasons, actually, though all linked by a common thread – and that is, education for tomorrow.

This book was written in the hope that there might be a little nugget of value for entrepreneurs venturing into education; for teachers hoping to bring in change, and for parents who want the world for their children. In short, anyone deeply invested in education as a concept and practice.

The first thing we did was make sure that we didn't remain ivory tower theorists. While committed to giving shape to our ideas, we have tried our best to provide the children of Oakridge an empowering environment; their parents a worthy partnership; our team members work satisfaction, and those who invested in our dream, a robust return.

Those of you who have kept us company through the twenty-odd chapters of this book would have surely figured out by now that Raj, Shomie and I are committed optimists. At the core of this optimism is the belief that, as far as school education goes, we can make tomorrow better than today.

As Shomie says, we look forward to a tomorrow where, within enabling regulatory frameworks created by governments, edupreneurs can empower teachers to be facilitators.

In this journey we have learnt much more than we can possibly teach but, perhaps, the most important lesson we imbibed is that conversations – however incidental or improbable – can lead to change. And small changes can have a ripple effect with significant impact.

This book is also an attempt to acknowledge all those who walked with us as we followed and enabled a path. Fittingly, that path was imagined by Shomie Das, the man who saw tomorrow.

Acknowledgements

This journey of more than three decades that I have written of in this book, filled with numerous highs and lows, would not have been possible without the support of many unsung heroes. There are so many of them that failing to express my gratitude would leave this book incomplete.

Although Raj and I are the lead characters, the real action belongs to our directors Prasanna Mandava, Sitaram Tummala, Dvrk Prasad, Sreeni Dasari, and K.V.V. Satyanarayana. Our senior leadership team, including Challaiah Choudary, V.N.N. Murthy, Rakesh Gupta, Sumit Handa, Sridhar Vangala, Sunita D., JNR, K.P. Panakala Rao, and many more, have stood by us nearly from day one. Our principals, including Ms Adilakshmi, K.V. Arjun Rao, Hema Sanjay, Hema Chennupati, Ramanjit Ghuman, and Jyothi Reddy, though not mentioned in the book to keep it concise, have made equal contributions. My office team, Kholi Kayedini, Srinivas Grandhala, Mahesh L., and Sandhya Nandyala, supported me in numerous indispensable ways.

I am blessed to have a diverse group of people who wholeheartedly wished for our success. Family comes first on that list: Yarlagadda Nagamuneswara Rao, Tummala Venkateswara Rao, Radhika, Anita, Parvataneni Srinivasa Rao, Dr Dasari Mohan Prasad, Myneni Padmaja, Saibabu, and others.

Our list of well-wishers is as lengthy as this book. Nonetheless, some names must be mentioned without fail, including Balarama Krishna Talasila, Nagabushanam Kommareddy, Lakshminarayana K., and Pydah Krishna Prasad.

While our journey was enriched by many luminaries and generous individuals, some of whom I have named here, writing this book was a significant endeavour in itself.

It all started with my friend Lalita Iyer, who encouraged me to undertake this project. I am immensely grateful to her for her encouragement, for spending hours with Shomie and me to facilitate our discussions, record conversations, transcribe the content, and give shape to it. Sumit Dasgupta and his team – Sukanya Das, Ananda Sen, and Ramona – gave the final shape to this book on the foundation laid by Lalita. Their contribution is invaluable. Special gratitude goes to Andrew Otis, who urged us to undertake some significant rework.

Finally, the three main people in my life – my mother, the late Anjana Devi, my daughter Vindhya, and my son Vishal – have played a significant role in inspiring, shaping, and supporting me in every possible way to become who I am today. They are the reason and source of strength that enabled me to share this story with you all.